"In this uncertain, topsy-turvy [illegible] journey to find peace in every p[illegible] Peace, Donna Melanson courageously lays bare her soul with powerful, authentic, and raw honesty and emotion so that you can discover new joy, peace, and fulfillment. No one can be loved until they let themselves be seen. No one can be seen until they learn to love themselves. You will LOVE traveling with Donna as she guides you to self-love along YOUR path to peace."* **Brian Biro, America's Breakthrough Coach**

"Donna's perseverance and ongoing inspiration in her book - A Yogi's Path to Peace, may just be the book to inspire you on your journey. Each one of us needs a strong foundation and Meditation is a simple nonobtrusive tool to equip us with all that we need to lead a balanced happy and healthy life." **Bawa Jain, Secretary General, World Council of Religious Leaders**

"Donna Melanson's story as chronicled in A Yogis Path to Peace, helps one see that our life truly is a journey of self-discovery. Both full of pain and challenge, and success and joy. Finding the strength to peel back the mistruths we acquire and accept, to find the place of being and sharing at our core, is the mission we all have. Donna's unflinching honesty in sharing her path can inspire us all. Thank you, Donna!" **Swami Babarama of Kashi Ashram, Florida.**

"Donna has crafted a beautifully honest and extremely helpful book with engaging stories about her own journey that will lift you up while pointing the way to your own liberation. Broken down into three sections, this is an easy and uplifting read that is timely for anyone looking to manifest more inner peace." **Paul Samuel Dolman, Podcaster - What Matters Most, and Author of Hitchhiking with Larry David**

A YOGI'S PATH TO PEACE

MY JOURNEY TO SELF-REALIZATION

DONNA MELANSON

A Yogi's Path to Peace: My Journey to Self-Realization

Library of Congress Control Number: 2020917460

Publisher's Cataloging-In-Publication Data
(Prepared by The Donohue Group, Inc.)

Names: Melanson, Donna, author.
Title: A yogi's path to peace : my journey to
    self-realization / Donna Melanson.
Description: [Boca Raton, Florida] : Yellow Pineapple
    Publishing, [2020] | Includes index.
Identifiers: ISBN 9781735452906 (paperback) | ISBN
    9781735452944 (hardback) | ISBN 9781735452913
    (ePub) | ISBN 9781735452920 (mobi)
Subjects: LCSH: Melanson, Donna. | Yogis--United States--
    Biography. | Yoga--Psychological aspects. | Mind and body. |
    Meditation--Psychological aspects. | Self-realization. |
    LCGFT: Autobiographies. | Self-help publications.
Classification: LCC BL1238.54 .M45 2020 (print) | LCC
    BL1238.54 (ebook) | DDC 294.5/436092--dc23

YELLOW PINEAPPLE
PUBLISHING

Printed in the United States of America
First Printing

This book was written for all the beautiful souls of the world.
May you, too, find peace.

CONTENTS

PREFACE

Anyone who has ever taken a yoga or meditation class has experienced a wide variety of instructors who often say things that are meant to inspire – most are wonderful and uplifting bits of wisdom. Others just leave students scratching their heads wondering who this woo-woo person is and why they ended up in their class. There's even a hashtag #shityogateacherssay that posts some of the funniest memes, reminding me, a 500-hour RYT (Registered Yoga Teacher) that I always need to think before spouting wise words to a class – or at least make them laugh and pivot into a segment of laughing yoga to quell the silliness.

One day in 2014, I wandered into a yoga class in Boca Raton and finally met my yoga teacher soulmate. Donna Melanson was standing there putting up her hair. She wasn't dressed in matching designer yoga clothes. She wasn't wearing make-up or tons of jewelry – just a beautiful wedding band. And then she ever so quietly called the class to order and had us start in child's pose. She talked about setting an intention and in case we didn't have one we could use hers. That's the first time I heard, "I flow through life with ease and grace." I'd come home! Those words, Donna's presence and the practice were just what I was searching for.

I followed Donna around town to classes at different studios. To piece together a living from teaching yoga instructors are nomadic at least they were until the onset of COVID-19. The gentleness and peace she exuded was contagious – I had to get more of whatever Donna had by attending every class she offered. As two introverts we were a great match once we overcame our shyness and started hanging out together outside of class. Donna welcomed me into her home and her extended family. Having just lost my mother it was wonderful to relax into the embrace of her clan.

After nearly a year practicing with Donna, she announced her first Teacher Training Course under her own company, Azul Yoga. It didn't take much to convince me to sign up, though it was for my own growth – I didn't have a single idea about ever teaching a class. Taking classes with Donna had already changed my life, eased my pain, calmed my trauma and transformed this type-A entrepreneur into a much better version of myself.

Nine months later a yoga teacher was born. We studied intensely, anatomy, the sutras, each and every limb of yoga and discussed it among a group of women who I am honored to call my friends and fellow teachers. Donna shared everything she knew, and we ate it up like chocolate. Always calm, gentle and yet firm about our studies, we learned to teach from our heart and soul, sharing our love for yoga with students instead of standing before them like those long-ago ballet teachers who rapped our shins with a cane when our turnout wasn't perfect. It wasn't about perfection or competition we learned, each day would be different, each body would be different, Donna told us.

My only regret is that I didn't keep a notebook next to me during practice. Donna so often said something that I wanted to remember. At times I did keep my phone near, on silent, and furtively typed in whatever morsel of wisdom I could. "Just show up and do the best you can with what you've got today." "Just be, just be, just be." I could go on and on. So many of Donna's words flow out of me today when I teach. The best homage I can pay her is to teach in a natural and serene way without artifice or contrivance. No crap-filled sentences that make one go hmmmm. Keeping it real in every way – that's the greatest lesson that came from what I coined as The Melanson Method.

Knowing Donna's story of how she came to the mat. Learning from her how to come to my own mat and know that yoga and meditation work – truly, work is what Donna shares with us here in "A Yogi's Path to Peace: My Journey to Self- Realization." We live through the heartbreak of many years and the joy of her children. We walk with her up the mountain where she hears the words, "yoga, yoga, yoga" chanted softly through the wind. We cry with her, we laugh with her and we find peace with her as she discovers yoga and meditation and then shares the bounty and beauty with us. We rejoice when she meets Mike, her fabulous husband. I'd clone him for every single woman I know. We watch as Donna turns from the classroom to broadcasting live every morning from the beach on Periscope – gentle yoga, meditation and sangha (aka community) a place for her peeps to gather and chat. She holds that space daily and shares it freely along with "The Silent Bit," her podcast featuring other yogis and lessons in the chakras and so much more. And now, you hold in your hands her memoir. As her friend and forever student I am proud of the person she is, the writer she's become and her drive to share her goodness, her love and peace with the world. Let's join her in the circle of love and together we can wish that all beings, everywhere, be happy and free.

Om shanti,
Dindy Yokel
August 4, 2020
Boca Raton, FL

INTRODUCTION

Yoga is the union of the body and mind guiding us to the awareness of the trues essence of who we are. As we go deeper into the practice, we move on a journey of self-discovery, we come to realize that most of our thoughts that become actions are all based on stories -- some of them real, some of them perceived.

I had a conversation the other day with a friend. I was trying to shift her thoughts to the possibilities of life, instead of her current state of affairs. I told her to hold the thought, that the right man is coming her way. She responded *"If you say so. I think I'm destined to be alone. I can't take anymore bullshit and pain."* And, so it is... I thought to myself. If that's what you truly believe, then that's what you'll have.

Belief is a very powerful energy that has the ability to warp or define our perspectives, to decimate one's grip on reality, or make one soar to new heights, to cause great harm or create miracles. We know this but we're not thinking about that as we're living through a crisis or trying to change our life. We simply get stuck in the story that we're telling our self.

The stories we tell may be true but are they true because of the self-perpetuating story that we keep repeating, like my friend's story, that has her destined to be alone. When will we begin realizing that perhaps these beliefs are negative and contribute to a false narrative that limits happiness and keeps us from living our truth?

In this book I share my life so you can see what it looks like to change the way you think in order to change the way you live, in three parts.

Part one - Know Yourself: To become conscious you have to look at yourself in your entirety. Here are the stories that I told myself about myself, because to begin anything, you need to begin where you are. Through self-study and digging deep into habits, patterns, right perception, misperception, and the awareness of all things.

Part two – Love Yourself: Demonstrates how I cleared a path to living my best life through journal entries, blog posts, positive statements and yoga.

Part three – Be Yourself: Is living my truth, which leads me to peace and happiness, and how you can do it too! We are healed when we live our truth, and when we heal ourselves, we help heal the world.

I would like to acknowledge that we are going through big changes right now, as COVID changes our way of being. Many people are living through a crisis, trying to change their lives, and are bitter about the unfairness of it all. My desire to write my story came from a deep-seated feeling that somehow my story could help, but since this is my story and from my perspective, I've changed the names of the people in it.

I've had many people help me along the way, even when I felt there was no one; Susan, Robert, Kathy, Dennis, Joyce, Bill, and Beth - thank you. High praise to my parents for giving me the best childhood; to my husband for his love and unwavering support, and to our children and grandchildren who continually inspire me.

I want to acknowledge my Azul Yoga community on periscope.

tv who motivate me to keep going, and send gratitude to my gentle readers who gave me gentle corrections that needed to be made. A big shout out to A. Kelly, Dindy Yokel, Theresa Linhart, Bailey Minish, Megan Minish, Joyce Leach, Andrea Woodburn, Terri Stewart, and all who helped bring this book to completion.

PART ONE
KNOW YOURSELF
The Stories that We Tell

KNOW YOURSELF

BEGINNING WHERE I AM
CIRCA 2009

I feel relief in my failure, and I'm embarrassed and ashamed, not only of the failure, but of the relief felt. I've been living in a world created by someone else's narrative of who I should be. Repressing who I am on the inside, dutifully doing all of the things expected of a good person on the outside. Keeping to a script that I had no hand in writing.

In some situations, this can be a very good thing, like keeping it together as a parent when you are mentally broken or being a good spouse when, inside, you just want to run away from all the pressures of domestic responsibilities. It comes in handy, however, when trying to keep the peace, like respectfully listening to your father's thoughts on how the world should be when you disagree with him most of the time.

In other situations, it can lead to a bit of an identity crisis. In the past, when I've felt confident in accomplishing a goal, I've been surprised by the people who doubted me. When I doubt myself, I'm confused when people believe I can do things. I think people just don't know who I am. Indignant, shouldn't I know myself best? The truth is, I'm just figuring it out for myself.

Most of my life, I've felt that I've put a false face on everything. Thinking that I know how the other person feels, and not wanting to feel stupid, weak, needy, or my greatest concern over the past ten years - pathetic. I know when to be quiet or to keep the peace by saying one of my slightest truths that validates what another is saying, that makes it seem that I agree.

I'm not sure how all this happens, or where it comes from, but I've noticed that other people do it too. This desire controlled or not, to jump on the bandwagon and strengthen someone else's argument. Is it a basic need to be liked, or something more, that makes us join the masses in singular thought?

The irony of this is that I have this insatiable desire to let the world know who I am and what I've been through, feeling as if my story can make a difference in the world. While writing under a pseudonym and avatar image as Goldilocks Blog – with the tagline of "searching for" "having" or "creating" a perfect life in a perfect world, depending on what day you're reading.

I've spoken to a few friends and a few acquaintances about it, totaling about ten people, but of those ten people, I've only told about five what the actual blog site's name is. My guess, since I'm trying to figure myself out, that it's probably because I feel like it's false. Goldi, short for Goldilocks, is who I want to become and is not actually me yet.

Or maybe she is me, like what comes first, the chicken or the egg, and the hiding comes from not feeling the credibility to say these truths and being this cheesy cheerleader of sorts; after years of being worn down, overworked, sad, and facing my total financial demise.

I'm also middle age, single, and practically jobless as a real estate agent in the height of a recession. I'm so close to a nervous breakdown that most days, I have to remind myself to breathe. There's so much uncertainty, like will I be able to keep my car.

I need to shift into the life I want to be living because I can't keep living this way. So, to start, I make myself get up and get moving. I begin by taking myself to the one hundred acres of land, located just outside of Asheville, NC, that for the moment I still own.

From my home I travel forty-five minutes by car to the area of woods I plan to hike. I drive up a hill and park next to the old over-grown cemetery. I open the door and step outside to a green grassy knoll, and as I do, the breeze smacks me in the face as if to wake me up, welcoming me to life. I instantly and surprisingly feel more alive than I have in more than a decade.

With my new awareness, I begin looking around, noticing the beauty of nature, and breathing in deeply, as I feel the need to take it all in, hyper-aware of the golden sun shining overhead in the bright blue Carolina sky.

I walk to the opening in the woods. The trailhead is lined with wildflowers - yellow, purple, and white, and I notice trees of all sizes. As I walk further, heading deeper into the woods, the trees start getting bigger, taller, and wider. Under this thick canopy of trees, it becomes darker with just a few beams of light making their way through the branches. The wind blows, causing the shadows of the leaves to dance across my path.

Further up the trail, I notice a large grey rock. It's about the size of a small car, and as I get closer, I see that a rich green moss is covering one entire side. A spring is near. I hear the water trickling over smaller patches of rocks nearby, and with just a few more steps, I see the water from the stream as it moves across my path. I step over, the flow of water is only a few inches wide, but I notice the dark fertile soil around it is wet. I pause, as I marvel at the beauty nature, self-sustaining, feeding itself.

The path begins to climb in elevation. I feel so peaceful here, feeling so totally and fully present in the moment, and these feelings only strengthen the deeper I go and the higher I climb. It seems magical in the sense that the peace and yes, love too, that's in the air, feels palpable. I feel completely safe, even though wild cats and black bears roam these mountains. I feel as if I am one with all.

I keep walking. I keep climbing in elevation as the path climbs to the left and then back to the right. I keep moving forward zig zagging my way up the mountain, and as I near the top, I see that the old path ends. If I want to get to the top of this mountain, I'm going to have to use my hands to climb up those last few feet, so I do. I make it to the top of this mountain ridge where it's level and expansive and sunny. I take a deep breath in, and I bask in the light.

I walk closer to the opposite edge of this mountain and look down below. I catch sight of a river gracefully winding through the base. I look up and spot the most amazing vista of peaks and valleys for as far as the eye can see.

I perceive the vastness of the sky, still feeling this connection to all, overwhelming, I begin to sense this grateful feeling of being alive.

I breathe it all in.

Over the next few months, I come back as often as I can to be alone with the strength and steadiness of the mountain, the majesty of the trees, in harmony with the gentle sounds of the rustling leaves—the perfect backdrop for the birds to sing their song.

I'm still surprised by the amount of freedom that I feel here. My body feels lighter. I'm not sure anyone would believe me, I'm not sure I believe me, but this land is healing me. I feel different here. I can't put it into words - I don't want to lose this feeling. I hesitate to leave because I haven't felt this good in so, so long.

As I continue walking the land, I start hearing a chant in my head: yo-ga, yo-ga, yo-ga, sounding like the chant of to-ga, to-ga, to-ga, in the movie *Animal House* being recited with real earnestness. And, it's strange that I hear this because I don't feel like I know anyone who practices yoga, or know where I can practice yoga, but I have this incredible urge to practice yoga at the top of this mountain.

Stranger still, the only yoga I remember was from a class in a community center that I took with my mother when I was around eight. Nonetheless, the voice keeps repeating.

I must have spoken out loud about the fact that I want to practice yoga at the mountain top, because a few weeks later, a friend gives me a hot pink foam yoga mat, which is way too small for my 5'8" body, and a VHS recording of a half-hour gentle yoga class that's set on a white sand beach.

I begin to practice this recording daily at home, and I notice that I feel so great after the yoga, so calm, so quiet, so still. Innately, I begin to sit up and meditate after the practice. It might be because I'm not ready to let this good emotion go, almost like it's a drug I'm addicted to or a craving for something sweet.

I don't want to get up. I just want "to be," because it's the only moment outside of the time spent on the mountain that I perceive peace. Some days I sit and meditate for just a few minutes, and some days I sit for an hour.

I feel more grounded, and with a coffee beside me, I start journaling. I try to write on three separate subjects. First, I journal on whatever comes to mind and flows out of me. Second, I write in the present tense as if it's already true about how happy I am with my now perfect life.

I'm writing about the life I want to be living, then I write my blog post for the day, hoping to continue on with positive thoughts and the desire that I can inspire others to do the same.

I can't be the only one suffering, and I somehow honestly believe that this daily practice will change my life. I need to flood myself with good news, good thoughts, and good energy. I can't handle anything else.

I had a dream last night. I was in a store and holding up a long line of people wanting to check out, but when I finished, no one was behind me. As I gathered my belongings, I noticed that I had the clerk's journal of transactions. I handed it back to her, and she thanked me.

Outside, I could see a vacant lot across the street where a house once stood. I could see people milling about, and I walked towards them. Children were running around, and one of them was playing with animal skins that were left to warm the people who stayed through the night. It disturbed me, but the child seemed happy.

I sat down on the curb in front of this empty lot and turned to my right. A couple is sitting next to me. I assumed they were homeless, and at that moment, I wonder if I am too.

THE STORIES THAT WE TELL
Circa 1988 - 1998

I woke up this morning with the feeling of blankness. It's the first night in our home as man and wife. I have this substantial sinking feeling as I lay awake next to Keith, the man I'm going to be with for the rest of my life, wondering if I just got married because all my friends were already married, and so, maybe, did I just want to get married too?

Do I really love him that much, or was it on the list of things I should do by my age? The thoughts and heavy feelings run through me, wondering, *what have I done*? It feels as if I just woke up next to a stranger, and I guess he kind of is. I've only known him for a few months. I feel a distance or a disconnection from him, and it doesn't seem like he really cares, or maybe he does care, and I just can't read him, or perhaps he's lying there thinking the same thing as me.

In my mind, Keith is "the good guy," which I know is why I married him. He's 6' -1", thin, has short-cropped light brown hair, and hazel colored eyes. He always dresses conservatively and neatly. He's funny and has a mild manner about him. He never raises his voice, seeming to always be calm and sheepishly cool.

He's non-confrontational, and if I'm honest, really kind of blank. I love him, but I do find that I love all people. One time when my girlfriends and I were chatting about our likes and dislikes of boys, they became silent when I simply stated that I could date anyone. I can find something to love in every guy. It makes me wonder if it's a character flaw in me.

Keith and I were married on a cruise ship while docked in the Port of Miami, before beginning our three-day two-night cruise. We planned for the wedding to be out in the open on the deck of the ship, but because of rain, it was performed under an awning on a landing that led inside.

During the middle of the ceremony, after a terrible and extraordinarily long and loud "WAAAA" horn sound, an announcer, whose voice blared through the intercom that was located directly over our heads said, "Attention crew - passengers will be boarding shortly."

Keith, my soon to be husband, wouldn't look me in the eyes as we said our vows, and for some reason I felt so awkward and nervous in front of the fifteen witnesses that were present. A nervous smile came across my face, and I honestly believed that I might laugh.

Our officiant was an older woman dressed in a lavender and deep purple combination of a polyester skirt and shirt. She finishes the ceremony, we kiss, and we move inside to a small wood-paneled room. Off to the side is a table set up with a small round single-layer cake with yellow icing and orange trim.

It's topped by a small statuette of a cutesy cartoonish looking couple. Next to it is one bottle of champagne and a few glasses, not enough glasses or champagne for the fifteen of us. The room is nice but is devoid of anything else that would suggest it's set up for a wedding celebration, and with fifteen people watching, my father suddenly asks me to dance.

There is no music playing.

I don't want to leave my father hanging there with his hand extended out to me, with this huge and very, unexpected gesture of his. He's the guy that doesn't go anywhere. He's the guy that just sits on the couch and watches sports; in fact, he watches three televisions at the same time, all tuned to different sporting events. I'm surprised that he even knows that people dance at weddings.

Then, he starts humming as I take his hand. This situation is totally awkward for me, compounded by the fact that I'm an introvert, who doesn't want to stand or speak, much less dance in front of anyone.

I'm wondering - who is this man? When horrifyingly, my mother jumps in and starts humming the same song. Apparently, she knows it too; I don't. The whole situation is compounded by the fact that they are, in fact, recently divorced after twenty-five years of marriage.

Neither of them can carry a tune, and my father and I are not good dancers. We're slow dancing, and we seem to keep moving in a circle. I'm getting dizzy, and it's all just - wrong. Luckily a photographer walks in after ten excruciating minutes, where my father has now been encouraging my husband and me to dance. It has seemed like an eternity.

I've invited my mother, father, brother, grandmother and one friend. We had said we would keep the wedding small, inviting only our immediate family, since we didn't have money to spend. Keith has invited a few of his friends to come down from North Carolina and proceeded to go out for a bachelor party the previous night, somehow ditching my brother in the process. While at the same time, I stayed home with our mothers and grandmothers.

An announcement comes over the intercom an hour later, instructing all passengers who are not sailing, that it's time to depart. We head to our room, where I notice for the first time that Keith is hungover.

A year and a half later, I give birth to a son, Max. I believe he's the most beautiful baby boy in the whole wide world, and two years later, I give birth to our daughter Ally, the most beautiful baby girl. I guess all mothers feel that way about their child, I say, smiling with the pride of a mother, and I love that the three of us share blue eyes and blond hair. But what is truly remarkable is how much love I feel for them. I didn't know it was even possible to love this much. It's such a strong and powerful connection that runs so deep. I just didn't know love could feel this way.

My husband and I are struggling financially. I don't know how we're doing it. On paper, it doesn't add up, but somehow, we manage to have food and pay our bills. We've started doing some extra work for a charity. It doesn't pay much, but it helps, and we can bring the children with us.

A few years later, we borrow money from my dad. Keith and a friend start a side business in tree trimming. They buy a truck and chipper and a few chain saws. They price jobs at night after work, and on weekends they cut down the trees. It's given us a little bit of freedom where now we can visit my family and a few friends in Florida.

Although instead of making me feel better, I'm starting to feel a little resentful as I watch my friends live a way more comfortable life, while we're continuing to struggle. It's hard to take. Both of us have become all work and no play, and I'm sad and tired all the time.

I don't feel like I have the support of Keith or anyone here, he travels for work, my family is in Florida, and I feel alone. I have the children whom I love with all my heart, but it's hard never having a break as a parent. Keith and I are more like partners in life, who don't fight, and occasionally do things together.

Christmases, birthdays, and anniversaries are never celebrated with any gifts. Granted, we don't have the money, but I always manage to get Keith something. I begin looking for a new career, maybe that will make me happy. My bachelor's degree in Interior Design is not in big demand here. The downtown in Asheville is basically boarded up. We keep sacrificing, however, to make a better life.

Later with Keith's support, I begin taking a few classes at the University, and I've received notification that I've been accepted into Physical Therapy Assistant School. But I don't think I can take it all anymore. This feeling of being unloved and alone, and when Keith comes home that day, I tell him that I'm not happy. I want a divorce.

He replies, "You just made the best day of my life, the worst day of my life. I just found out that Jack is going to sell me his Food Brokerage Business." Jack had started the business as a retirement project, but it's gotten too big, he wants to sell. Keith says excitedly, "And he'll owner finance."

He said those words to me so passionately, in a way I've never seen him so passionate. It has always been his dream to own his own brokerage someday. I am, however, taken aback and still stuck in the loop that's playing in my head, when he said it was the worst day of his life. I assume it's because I want to leave, and that's all it took.

That simple little acknowledgment that I mattered to him mattered to me, and with that, we turned over a new leaf. I decide not to enter the Physical Therapy program. We can't do both, and I agree to help him run the business, which is fine with me. I don't feel too bad. He's been dreaming of owning a food brokerage company for a long time, and my desire to be a Physical Therapist is new.

It feels like we are on the same path now, and I have hope of a better future. I ask my father and my stepmother if we can borrow money from them once again, this time to pay our bills for a few months until funds start coming in. They're taking a risk on us, and we feel like we're risking everything, even though what we have isn't much.

We sell Keith's twenty-year-old boat, buy him three new business suits, and we are on our way. I'm happy that I stayed in the marriage and I'm happy with him. I do believe he's a good man, maybe just not good at showing me. Soon Keith's traveling more than ever, leaving on Sunday nights and coming home Wednesday or Thursday night. I'm running the business out of our house.

We now have several men working for us traveling all over the southeast. I work at local stores and do all of the bookkeeping for the business, invoicing, payroll, buying cars for our employees, etc., as well as taking care of the children and everything around the house. My housework duties include painting the house, blacktopping the driveway, and mowing the yard. The children and I eat as cheaply as we can, and I make sure Keith has enough cash on him to entertain the district managers that he runs into, and for whatever else he needs.

Since I'm handling all the money now, I don't want him to feel like he has to ask permission. I know how that feels. I didn't like it when I had to ask. We're both working really hard, it is a genuine family effort, and it's starting to pay off. Our business is growing by leaps and bounds.

Keith wants to have more children, but I've been way past max capacity for years now. I can't physically or mentally do anymore, and I know I won't have any help. I'm seriously, beyond exhausted. I was tired before we started the business. Since Keith is never home, I always feel like a single working parent. I barely get to shower. Now it's even worse.

On weekends when he comes home, he drops his clothes on the floor of the bathroom upstairs, only for me to carry downstairs, to wash, dry and iron, and then for me to carry them all back up. He sits on the couch and watches TV exhausted from his week, but I'm exhausted from my week too. I know he's working hard though. Did I mention; our business is really growing?

Still, holidays, however, come and go with no presents. Once on Mother's Day, I suggested that maybe he should get me something. He responded by telling me I wasn't his mother.

On Saturdays, the kids and I go off to run errands, birthday parties etc. He does not cook, clean, take out the trash, or even pick up a plate off the table. He does, however, throw his napkin toward the trash, I guess that counts for something.

The children begin playing soccer. With no available coaches, Keith becomes the coach, and I became the team manager. I don't know what's going on, but I start having severe stomach problems.

Three years later, we move our business out of the house and into a warehouse where we start distributing products. I learn how to drive a forklift, supply and demand, and how to box and fill orders quickly. During the summers, the kids help fill the orders. It's surprising how good they are at such a young age. They never make a mistake.

I have a space set up for them in the loft of the warehouse with a sofa, TV, videos, and toys. My daughter starts a little newspaper that she sends to my father, her only subscriber, with most of the articles being about her brother and a few of the workers.

I'm getting excited because we've repaid my father and stepmom, and soon our business loan will be paid off to Jack, and we'll finally be able to reap the rewards of a job well done -maybe even hire someone else to lighten our load. I sell our home, for sale by owner, we move into an apartment, and start building our dream home.

I'm surprised at how happy I am to be using my degree again, and even though I barely have time to breathe, I'm excited to help design it, find the builder, arrange financing and deal with every other aspect of building our home. It truly is going to be my dream house.

It's in a new development in an exclusive area close to town. Keith and I go to an open house at the small pool clubhouse that's already been built. We meet other residents of the community, doctors and lawyers, and world travelers. Keith and I laugh later thinking that we're going to be their neighbors. We're still in a little basement apartment working our butts off. We haven't quite acclimated to the idea that we could be living the good life soon.

THE STORIES THAT WE TELL
Circa 1998

A year later, our new house is still not finished, and my life just changed by a look. I was sitting at my desk at the office, scrolling through a caller ID, looking for a number. My husband was at the office too, it was Friday, and he was heading out to make his weekly sales call at the corporate headquarters of the grocery store chain that purchased our products.

As he approached the door, I came across a name that I recognized but couldn't place. I looked up as he opened the door, and I said, "Do you know who Kimberly Mosakowski is?"

He stopped and looked at me in the eyes, seeming to scan for information. "Yes, she's a girl looking for a job... I'm trying to help her."

I detected a slight smirk across his face, and instantly I flashed to that unusual name coming up on our caller ID at our home office years ago. With nothing else being said, I immediately suspected a relationship, which was odd, because Keith is "the good guy."

He's not much of a gift-giver, or thoughtful, but I fully trust him. I've not been really happy, but I'd decided long ago just to write that off, that it's just the stage of life we're living; raising our children and sacrificing for our future. While other people are taking vacations, we're putting money back into our business and working. Plus, I never thought of him as the cheating type.

This weekend my son has an out of state soccer game. Keith is staying home and taking Ally to her soccer game. Max's friend who is also on his soccer team and lives in our apartment building with his father, has asked if his mom could come with us and share the hotel room that we booked. I don't know this woman, but I thought, why not? I know what it's like not to have enough money, and we're finally doing well enough.

As Lisa and I traveled down to South Carolina for the soccer game with the boys, we started talking and getting to know each other. For some reason I totally open up to her, confiding to her my fears, my hopes, my dreams. It may be because she's newly divorced, or maybe because she was a complete stranger, or perhaps it's because I finally have some time and someone to talk to. Regardless, for whatever reason, I tell her my whole story, including seeing Kimberly's name and of suspecting infidelity.

I learn that Lisa was once upon a time an Olympic swimmer, and for some reason this fact makes me crazy, super over-the-top excited. It may be because growing up in South Florida, I was a competitive swimmer. I practiced two hours a day before and after school for years, and then spent almost every weekend at swim meets. It wasn't a seasonal sport. It was year-round, and the Olympics to me was the only goal you had. And, even though I never even remotely came close, sitting next to her, I felt like, in a way, I had.

Lisa has been going through some tough times herself, with her divorce and with not having custody of her children. She hinted at some other things that she doesn't elaborate on. When I suddenly remembered that I have a book in my car that the author Brian Biro, an international speaker who's also a parent from my daughter's soccer team, had written and given to me as a gift for managing the team.

Joyful Spirit - How to Become the Happiest Person you Know! I had read it and enjoyed it and thought that it could help her. I also felt that it was very serendipitous, because Brian, the writer, had been a very successful swim coach at one of the largest swim clubs in California. In his book, he tells a few stories of lessons learned through coaching. I thought she's totally going to be able to relate.

Swimming had been such a huge part of my life growing up. It was more than just about sport, discipline, goal setting, or exercise, but it was a time in my life where I had time to just be with my thoughts. They were peaceful moments, and a time where I would come up with so many solutions. I never have time for any of that now. Maybe that's why I'm super excited to be talking to Lisa, with the good memories of the past. This unexpected connection to a part of my childhood at this time in my life, is a very welcome moment.

I thought back to when I was in eighth grade at the county championship, held at the Swimming Hall of Fame pool in Ft. Lauderdale, Florida. I was in the finals but seeded last. I'd just barely made it to the finals, and my dad was there and had been talking with one of his good friends, whose daughter also swam. His daughter, Susan was a rising star, but a recent car accident has left her paralyzed.

She was also there. My dad asked the two of them to speak to me about the techniques of my swimming stroke. At thirteen, I didn't really care about listening to any of that, I just wanted to be hanging out with my friends, but respectfully I listened, and probably more so because of the situation, and who they were.

After the conversation, I wheeled Susan around the pool deck. She was beautiful, popular, and four or five years older than I was. I'd been introduced to her two or three other times before, but I don't remember if we had ever spoken. As we moved around the pool deck, I became aware of the whispers, and the looks. It made me uncomfortable, even though I knew it wasn't about me. She seemed to handle it all with grace.

So, I had to ask, "How do you put up with all of these negative people?"

And she simply said to me, "Kill them with kindness."

That evening during the finals, I stepped up on that swimming block, feeling more real and present and grounded than I ever had before in my life. I felt no pressure. I was in the outside lane and not expected to win. I simply showed up, and as I dove into the water, I felt it, all of it. It was as if I dove into a different reality. I had an awareness of the conversation I had earlier that day about my swimming stroke and was fully present in the moment. I could feel the water all around me, pressing up against my hands. It felt as if I was in slow motion. I was light, and it was effortless. Like I had the ability to slow the video down and notice everything. Just me, awareness, and the water.

On the last turn, I happened to notice that I was ahead of everyone else. In the past, I would have doubled down and tried as hard as I could through will and determination, but for some strange reason, this time, I didn't. I just calmly and unaffectedly continued swimming. Aware of how my body was moving through the water, aware of my body breathing, aware of awareness.

When I finished the event, I had won! It wasn't just a win for me. It was a win for the team. Everyone was so surprised and excited, they were jumping all around me, congratulating me, but I felt just a little bit blank. Happy, I guess, but almost feeling like for that moment, I knew more than they did, and that the win they were celebrating, didn't really matter.

I don't know when or how I snapped out of that feeling. It didn't last long, but I still remember that moment, and how the water felt while swimming. Anyway, a week later, I get a call from Lisa. She says she needs to talk to me and asks if it is a good time. I hesitated but tell her it's fine. I think it was the tone of her voice that made me uncomfortable.

Lisa proceeds to tell me that while she was at her mother's house that day, she was thinking of me, as she sat outside with a cup of coffee and Brian Biro's book that I had given her. When a young guy who was renting her mother's garage apartment came downstairs, sat at the table with her, and said, he was really worried about a friend of his.

He said Kimberly had been having an affair with a married man for four years, that the man had just built a new house, and he proceeded to tell her many details that I had just told her about my life.

She said, "I think it's your husband."

I automatically begin to think that this woman is crazy. I mean, I just met her. Is she one of those people who just make things up to be closer to you? People are so weird. That can't be right.

So, I asked, "Well, how old is this woman?"

She said, "Twenty-one."

My mind wanders off searching my memories for the truth of this statement. I remember a college experience I had, when I told a sorority sister about her boyfriend cheating on her. She became mad at me and kept dating her boyfriend. She wasn't ready to hear it, I guess, I'm not sure. And I think I'm not sure if I am either.

We've moved into our new house, but it's been nine months since the moment in the doorway of the office that I've suspected he's cheating. For nine months, I've snooped, interrogated and questioned his every move. I actually can't believe that I need proof. I keep questioning myself. I'm not thinking clearly. He may not be perfect, but I believe he's mine. However, I have come to realize that I've met this Kimberly four years earlier, and I think she had to be twenty-one then.

We had a booth at a food convention, and I remember her so clearly because she looked beautiful, just like Julia Roberts in *Pretty Woman* after she's spent the night with Richard Gere's character: tall, with a short skirt and her natural long curly brown hair flowing. And, I know you're probably thinking that I'm just saying that because as a probably bitter wife, I want you to think she's a whore, but I'm not.

I kid you not, she looked beautiful just like Julia, but truth be told I don't really mind the other reference. Anyway, she kept coming over to our booth to talk to my husband. His Aunt was helping us work our booth and suggested that I should go over there near him. I told her that I thought Keith should handle it, but it did bother me. So later that day, remembering his Aunt's suggestion, I asked Keith to walk the convention with the children and me, thinking Kimberly would see us all together and back off. But, when we got close to the booth she was manning, he left us and walked over to her.

That night after the convention, not even a year into our new business, extremely tired with the extra work of the busy weekend, we chatted for just a moment about it before we fell asleep. He said, she's just a young girl who works up at headquarters.

The next day, he headed out of town.

Another month goes by after the call from Lisa. I find a new number, and embarrassingly I asked Lorelei, our only employee that's in the office with us, to call it for me, she does, and Kimberly answers.

That night I begin questioning Keith again about the new number for Kimberly and the phone call I had with Lisa, and all he keeps doing is redirecting the questions, asking "Who told you this." That's all he wanted to know, and all he wanted to say.

Finally, I asked, "How old is Kimberly."

He answered, "Twenty-one."

I then I knew that this woman was telling the truth, and at the same time, I still felt like it was unconfirmed. I'm not sure why.

Keith always had a story and an explanation for every question. This night, however, I will not let him go to sleep until he admits it. I lie, I tell him we'll never be able to make it work unless he tells me the truth. For some reason, I didn't trust myself. I didn't trust my gut. I didn't trust my intuition. I needed to hear it from him.

Maybe I'm just too worn down or incapable or unwilling to see the truth. Maybe I just want to be the good guy, so I need proof so that I can say, I am, in fact, the good person in this story. Or is it that maybe I'm just too busy moving through life, but I'm not really living it, to even know what's going on? So, I ask again; I need to hear it from him so that I'm beyond a shadow of a doubt - then I can leave.

Hours later, he admits the affair, and I agree to a counseling session that I know will never really matter.

THE STORIES THAT WE TELL
CIRCA 1960's, 70's, 80's

In the kitchen of the house of my youth, hung a black iron plaque, with raised white letters that said: "Behind every great man, is a woman telling him how to get there." I remember it so clearly because it hung next to the phone. This was when phones were attached to the wall, and sayings like this were everywhere.

In contrast, on the back of my brother's bedroom door was a sticker that read, "Male Chauvinist Pig." I read it often as my brother and I shared a fan in our non-air-conditioned house in South Florida. I would often sleep on the floor of his room, or try to, as in the stillness of the night all I could feel was heat and the sweat rolling down my skin. My mother said his attitude was somehow related to his experience with his female kindergarten teacher.

My favorite mantra at the time, was what I heard most often: "You can be anything that you want to be, an astronaut, or even President of the United States." Women's Lib, The Equal Rights Amendment, Title 9, were all just being implemented. But I was little, and for now, I was just happy playing in my make-believe world with my Barbies or acting out Cinderella for the umpteenth time with my friends down the street. My friends thought I was prissy with my blue eyes and blonde hair in pigtails, while often wearing a dress, innocently, skipping down the street singing la di da in my head.

At my grandmother's house, my imagination soared. She would tell me tales of her life growing up on a farm in Pennsylvania with her brother and sisters, coal miner father, and mother who grew flowers. She said they were gypsies, and she read our fortunes with cards. She also told me about her life later as a Vaudevillian Artiste, traveling throughout the United States and then settling down in New York City.

I could see myself, like her, traveling all over the country just like she did, and I knew when I grew up, I wanted to be like her in that respect. I would not sing or dance or act. I had none of those talents, and I was much too shy and introverted to try, but travel, that I could do. She talked about life in NYC and being swept off her feet by my grandfather in a limo, during the height of the depression, further fulfilling my girly make believe imagination of being rescued by a prince.

My grandfather, whom I've never met, had a sister who lived in Washington DC, and worked for the Federal Reserve Board for 40 years, at a time when most women didn't even work. To me, she represented class, status, dignity, self-respect, and culture. She was a modern woman.

I attended a small Catholic School that had no air conditioning in hot sunny South Florida, but I was somewhat used to that, as I said, we had no air conditioning in our home as well. The school had one class for each grade, Kindergarten through eighth grade. One morning I was sent to the principal's office because of my hair.

I was in about fourth grade, and I wanted to be different and unique. I'd spent a long time in front of the mirror that morning trying to create a new look. Brilliantly I thought I had achieved a hairdo that I had never seen as I parted my hair down the back of my head to my neck, like you would if you were putting your hair in pigtails. Instead of the pigtails, I pulled both sides in front and tied my hair underneath my chin. I was so proud of my new and distinct do.

My mother sold cosmetics out of the house. She was a go-getter, leading the state of Florida in sales. She also had the most consultants under her and was a leader around the country. And, she was beautiful and elegant and had a kind and quiet strength.

She must have seen the pride in my eyes, because she smiled, hugged me and sent me off to school with my new look. Once at school I was sent to the principal's office, where they chastised me and threatened to call my mother. They were shocked to hear that she already knew how I was wearing my hair, and instead made me take it down. My lesson that day was to conform, but a little seed was planted indirectly by my mother that day, that as far as she was concerned, it was okay to be different and creative, even if I failed.

In high school and college, I was on the homecoming court and was happy and relatively popular. Although I never won, I didn't give it, or anything for that matter, much thought. I just continued on in my "la di da" world, until my parents separated during my senior year of college.

I had attended a University in North Carolina because, at this point in my life, I still had not traveled anywhere. I'd never seen snow; I'd never seen the leaves change color; I'd never experienced a single fall day. My parents' separation, however, affected me way more than I expected. Not that I had everything that I'd ever wanted, but I guess I really never had anything bad happen to me before.

I always felt like I had basically everything I needed; a roof over my head, food, and friends. Upon graduation, not knowing how to handle this new situation, I, not willing to pick between parents, decided not to return home to Florida and stayed in North Carolina. It was easier this way, although I knew my interior design degree might not be as useful.

THE STORIES THAT WE TELL
CIRCA 2000

I told my soon to be ex-husband as we were ending our thirteen-year marriage by having the deepest conversations that we've ever had, that I always had this feeling that I was destined for some sort of greatness, he laughed as he replied, "You better get busy then."

I didn't like his reality checking response, but I remember wishing that we would have had more of those heartfelt discussions. It was the first time I ever felt a deep connection with him, where I thought it was real and honest and not just going through some rote course of life.

The conversation gave me a little pause where I reflected on our divorce. I've always believed that I could never be with a man that cheated on me, I have more self-respect than that, especially when you find out that the affair has been going on for four years. I think now, however, and I'm not proud of this, that if my husband's affair had just been in a moment of weakness and then it ended, that I may have been able to handle that, which really surprises me.

None of us are perfect - right, or I wonder, am I just that worn down. I always thought it was a zero-tolerance kind of thing, once you break the vows of commitment there is no more trust. Anyway, I guess I was just too busy to notice, but now, with awareness everything's starting to make sense, and perhaps there were other women.

One time, a few years into our marriage, the phone rang, it was a woman saying, did you know that your husband and so and so like each other. I asked him about it, and his response was, "It sounds like someone is jealous." I didn't know who he was talking about at the time if he thought *they* were jealous or if I was, but I let it go, probably because he didn't seem to react like he was worried about it.

Now I discover that the cash I had been handing Keith every week, was going to Kimberly - the beautiful and fifteen-years-younger-than-me Kimberly. I hate admitting how beautiful she is. I'm not sure if it would be better if she was old or ugly, but it just seems like it makes it worse. I'm only thirty-eight, and my mom and dad think I'm pretty.

It makes me feel really old, already being replaced by a much younger woman. I really begin to question everything about myself, and I've already been beating myself up for years. The funds that I thought were spent on district managers and salespeople etc. were used for Kimberly as she had been traveling with him, sunbathing by the pool, while the kids and I scrimped and worked, and worked, and worked.

What makes matters worse is apparently all of our employees have known about this relationship, and so do all the salesmen that live in this small town. His family knows about it too. So pretty much all the people I'm around all the time. The good news is, I finally now know and understand why his aunt gave us a book about relationships one Christmas, and why his friend's new wife asked me, "How do you trust Keith being out on the road so much?" I guess trying to bring me into awareness. It makes sense why Keith was mad at her. I only remember feeling sorry for her at that moment, thinking, poor girl that's no way to start a new marriage, and told her that I just do trust him fully. If I didn't, I wouldn't be able to be married to him.

Now I simply want the divorce to be over, I'm so over all this, and I want to have him as far away from me as possible, but now it seems he has more time than ever, and he's coming into the office every day. I can feel his presence; it feels like a dark cloud that somehow has weight to it that's continually moving towards me as

I force myself to sit still. Like punches to the gut all day long, every day, the blows feel continuous.

I want our children to have as small a scar as possible, so I feel I have to play nice, but these metaphoric gut punches are kicking my ass. I want to run away and leave. I want to take my children and go back home to Florida where I think I could have some support from family and old friends. My mom tells me that he doesn't deserve the children, but the children deserve a father.

She says this, I believe, because she grew up without a father, so I feel that she must really know. I think for a brief moment that Max and Ally would still see him in the summer months, but my mom's insistence makes me stay put. I feel with every bone in my body that I won't be able to take it. My gut is telling me to go. I feel it's heavy presence, and the continual punches, saying, "Leave, leave, leave."

It's easy for us to write a separation agreement for our personal lives, wanting the best for our children as our main goal. But we're struggling to come up with an agreement for the business. So, until that can be settled, we continue to run the business together. Keith insists that we sell our new house that we've only lived in for a few months for sale by owner, not because he will do any of the work, but because he knows I can and will handle it. It sells, and Keith buys a home.

I don't know where it comes, maybe out of habit of taking care of EVERYTHING, but I help Keith sell his car, while he goes out of town with Kimberly, and then help him get a new car and furniture etc. I set him up. I'm also buying a new home, but it turns out to be an undisclosed modular home. It's funny, I should have known better. I saw its construction.

I think one of the workers even said to me that they brought it in on a truck. But apparently, I'm still not listening, or paying attention to the signs. Maybe I have too much going on in my life that I don't have the ability to really understand what's going on around me. Or, maybe it was the antique front door that the builder put on that threw me off, I don't know, but I know it's not the house that I want to invest in. It's priced twice as much as what modular homes typically sell for.

I find myself and the children homeless, but with money, since we sold our home that we just built for a profit. Luckily, I get out of the contract for the undisclosed modular home. The kids and I check into a hotel, but now I have to move my stuff twice. I think we need a break, so I decide the kids and I are going to travel. I think that's one bright spot, in fact, I declare that we're going to make at least one trip a year.

Starting by going to see our friends Richard and Emma, and their three children in Austria. We met them while living in the apartments, although as it turns out Ally and their middle child Gemma were in kindergarten together, and Max and Sophie are in the same year. They have a younger son named Luke, and they all get along really well.

Richard and Emma were building a home at the same time as we were building ours, but Richard's job has brought them to Austria for a year. I'm excited to be going. It will be a great diversion. They're my favorite couple, and have been very supportive to me, even inviting Keith and me to spend that first Christmas with them after separating, for the sake of the children. Oh, I have such mad love for them, what a self-sacrificing and generous gift they gave us.

――――ᘛᘚᘛᘚ――――

We have great news for our business. We have two really big offers come our way. One is to merge our brokerage with another, making our brokerage the "go to" for private label products. The other is to start warehousing more products. The supplier has been having a hard time getting products to the stores.

We realize we need to warehouse those products ourselves or lose the brokerage on over one hundred and fifty items. We're excited about both the opportunities. It will bring more money into both of our houses and it will allow Keith to be out of the office that we're currently sharing.

After conversations with Keith, I line up an attorney to make the merger and new business happen, and when we go to sign, sitting in front of the attorney, papers in hand, Keith then says "I don't want to do this. I don't want to have less of the ownership in the new company than our partner, since he'll be splitting the other half with me."

I felt floored and gut punched again, wanting to be rid of him even more, if that was even possible. In the heat of the moment without really thinking, I trade full ownership of the brokerage, for full ownership of the distribution end of the business, just to have it over with and not have to see him on a daily basis. On one hand, it was good for my body and soul, but financially I was taking a big loss, and an even bigger risk. Now I'm without a home and I need to lease a bigger warehouse. Two big moves ahead of me.

The celebrated annual business party is here, for our most important client. I hesitate to go alone, but I feel the need to for business reasons. I need for everyone to see, in fact, I'M STILL HERE. Plus, I've always looked forward to this event in the past. I guess it's a girl thing, wanting to get dressed up. It's the only occasion I've been able to get dressed up for since graduating from college.

I'm feeling pretty good as I arrive, I'm a little nervous to see Keith and Kimberly there, but just that would have been welcomed, compared to the looks of pity I receive, and the conversations of sympathy that crush my resolve of standing strong. If I have to hear bless your heart one more time, I'm going to literally run out of this room screaming. But an amazing thing happens, Keith doesn't bring Kimberly, and I run into Brian.

Brian is a sales rep for bakery products. He's a few years older than me, very handsome and seems like he should be a model opposite a female model in a Lily Pulitzer dress. He lives in Charlotte, North Carolina and in this moment, I'm just so very grateful to be dancing. He asks for my phone number.

Today I received a letter from Brian. How sweet I think, nobody sends letters anymore. For six months now I've been seeing him once a month. We live two hours apart and this works, because I don't want to have anyone around the children unless it becomes something serious.

It's been nice to have someone to focus on, especially when your soon to be ex-spouse has someone, which I'm acutely reminded of on a daily basis when he calls and comes by for the kids, and every weekend at the soccer games. For some reason the thought of Keith knowing I'm alone week after week, makes me feel somehow - worse. Brian and I have plans to go to Vermont for New Years. It'll be nice, at least, to not be alone.

The letter, though, says that it's not working out between us. He's met another girl. He believes he wants to marry her. He tells me that she said to him, as she's lying next to him, that she just wants to breathe in him... (insert eye-roll here.)

It's another blow to the gut. I feel an urgent deep-seated need to be loved as I feel the hole within me growing wider. I've felt so empty for so long, in the marriage and, now, out of the marriage. It also has been hard not having the kids all the time. I have this habit of checking on them sleeping before I go to bed. Call it an OCD thing or whatever, but I feel like I can't sleep without them.

When I lost my marriage, I also lost the man whom I thought was my friend, his family, our friends together, and again most importantly our children part of the time. I feel as if I'm being punished over and over again, for something I didn't even do. Holidays I found out are the worst, sitting at home alone.

I've joined the gym. I need to do something to get rid of all of this anxiety. I went to the doctor, and he gave me some medicine, but my mother says I need to feel the pain. I think I just need a break from everything.

I take the medicine for a few weeks, probably not even long enough to feel any affects, but my mother's guilt makes me stop. I feel bad because I'm going to the gym after work, after quickly checking in on my children to make sure they're okay, and that they have food, etc. I feel guilty leaving them, but if I don't go and work out, I feel like I may literally explode.

It's been nice going to the gym. I'm finding that I'm seeing the same people, and eventually I begin to meet them. A man named Daniel asks me if I want to go to a baseball game with him and another woman I've met. I do, the game happens to fall on one of the two weekends that I don't have the kids, and I have to say that

I'm finding myself attracted to this tall, good looking doctor. He's somewhat mysterious, and I can't quite figure him out, but I find myself drawn to him in a very connected way.

Daniel and I start going out about once a month which works for me, and I'm still looking for a home, and running the expanded distribution company, as well as taking care of my sweet children. I love them so much. Daniel too is working really hard. He's in the process of opening up his own clinic. But I can't help noticing, like Brian, there is a pattern of only being able to date once a month, which seems odd even though we both are extremely busy. It was easy at first, but I find myself wanting him more, where with Brian I could take it or leave it. With Daniel, I can't seem to handle this feeling any longer of wanting him and not being able to have him. Something doesn't feel right.

I'm still in the middle of my divorce. In North Carolina you must be separated for a year before you can get legally divorced. I don't know why, but Keith doesn't want to lie and say that we're already been separated for a year. It's apparently not because he's ethical. I don't really want to ever do anything illegal or immoral, but in this case if he would've agreed, I would have too. I know we're never getting back together, and I feel like it's literally killing me. My body is always in this state of heaviness and sadness. If it wasn't for the children, I'm not sure I would even get out of bed.

In fact, the day after I had confronted Keith about the affair, and made him leave, Ally came into my bedroom at nighttime saying she was hungry. I realized then, that I had let the day go by without feeding my children. It was a real wakeup call and I decided in that moment that I had to focus on them; their happiness, their safety, their security. And, I've been trying to do that ever since.

DONNA MELANSON

I finally found a home that I love. It's perfect, it's in the neighborhood where we built our home that we just sold, near all the best schools, and it's been on the market for a long time. So, I believe I can get a good deal on it and make this house look great with a few cosmetic changes. I'll just remove all of the wallpaper, add a fresh coat of paint, and hardwood floors throughout in place of the five different types of flooring that you can see right when you walk into the house. I'm excited about using my design degree again. I really love being creative, and I believe I'll be able to make money on this house.

Months in a hotel have not been fun with two children. Like when we moved into a hotel that's next door to a summer soccer camp the kids can go to while I work, only to find out after that the camps are cancelled. This period of my life has been very stressful, juggling all the many aspects of life, so I'm especially grateful that we're finally moving into our new home, maybe now we can get organized and settled.

My demeanor, however, must be poor, because my wise eleven-year-old son, Max asked me why I'm allowing myself to suffer when no one else seems to be. I look at him blankly unable to answer, but feeling spent and empty after juggling the moves, the renovation, working full time, and being a single parent, while thinking of all the heartache that has come my way. He just can't understand at his age, and yet, at the same time, I know that he's right. I have become bitter. I'm supposed to be living the good life now.

A Christmas present for Kimberly is arriving late. Keith has the nerve to call and ask if he can have it delivered to my house because he works nearby. A present of all things, A PRESENT! I want this divorce with Keith over ASAP. It's a constant reminder of something I don't want to be reminded of, why does it have to drag on soooo long, WHYYYYY, I cry, is it taking longer than a year. I let Daniel go, I just can't take it all, and I regret it for a very long time.

Keith and Kimberly are traveling, and through one of the vendors, I hear they are going to the Super Bowl, which incites me in anger. I become even more resentful because I, not Kimberly was the one who was supporting Keith's dream of the Food Brokerage. I was taking care of the children, the household, and the business. It was, my dad's money for goodness sake.

Sacrificing in every way possible, and now seeing someone else reap the rewards of that effort is just more salt in the wound; more punches to the gut. I've stopped working out. Because when I do go to the gym, I see Daniel. It just makes my heart hurt more. That feeling of wanting someone and not being able to have them.

I am the one who ended it with Daniel, but it wasn't because he was smothering me with love and affection and constantly wanting to see me. It was because he didn't seem to have time for me. I didn't feel like a priority in his life and felt almost like I was supposed to feel grateful for the sacrifice he made, to spend that one day a month, that he so graciously carved out of his schedule. And maybe, I should have felt grateful that I had anyone in my life, but after feeling alone in my marriage, I'm not quite capable of being alone in any relationship, plus now I'm even busier than ever.

With all of my nonexistent free time, I've decided to open up a vitamin store. I've been warehousing most of the items I would need already, and I think it would be a good way for me to get rid of some

DONNA MELANSON

of the surplus that lingers there. Keith and my dad think it's a terrible idea, which makes me determined to do it more.

I hire Justin to run the store. He's a young biology major who's been traveling around the United States working odd jobs, trying to find himself. I don't tell him, but I heard him sing and play the guitar, and he reminds me of Justin Timberlake, in the way he looks, and in the way he sounds. He's a godsend for sure, he's personable and charming, and I think I may even ask him to teach Max and Ally how to play the guitar.

Speaking of the children a funny thing happened the other day. The kids and I went to do our weekly grocery shopping. When we came upon the cookie aisle, Max and Ally begged me to buy some Oreo cookies. I told them "No" as I have for whatever reason a real weakness for Oreo cookies.

I told them that they know if we buy the Oreo's that I will end up eating them all, and that they are allowed to pick out any other cookies they want. They were, however, insistent that I buy the Oreo's and begged and promised that they would hide them if I bought them, so I did, trusting them as I looked into the beautiful blue eyes of those cute innocent faces.

That night when I went to sleep, rolling over to my stomach for comfort, I slid my hands underneath my pillow to support my head and found the package of cookies. Where Max, my jokester son had hidden them. It was really nice to laugh before I fell asleep. I sure do love my children.

THE STORIES THAT WE TELL
Circa Now

As I continue to write the stories that I had told myself, the guru in me can't help but reflect on what I would say to the student who is me. What wisdom can I impart up to this point. What's most important as you begin your journey of self-study?

To become conscious, you must look at yourself in your entirety. Acknowledge where you are starting from, with the perspective of detached awareness. Aware of stories you're telling yourself about the family you were born into. Aware of your stories about the unfairness of your life. Aware of limiting beliefs. Aware of your thoughts that are happening right now, and most importantly aware of all the good that's around you.

You must begin where you are, with no judgements. This is what we can control. This moment right now. The thoughts that you are having and the emotions that you are experiencing right now. Not what has happened in the past. Not what you are concerned about for the future. Not what we may be falsely assuming right now! You must find your grounding, your root, while examining your thoughts as an objective observer.

Exercising the mind like this takes great effort, but soon you begin to realize the stories that you tell yourself are just words that make up a story. It's the meaning that you give the narrative of your childhood, of your marriage, of not trusting your instincts, or of whatever it is that your telling yourself, that affects you. Aware that you don't have to stay stuck in the story that you're in, aware that you can create a new one.

Know your story but know it's not all of your story. Notice that I don't write more about my children. I'm not writing about all of the good that they bring into my life. "My story" is mostly about "poor me," how much can I take, not knowing at the time that what you focus on you get more of, so this self-perpetuating prophesy continued.

So, I must ask you now – Do you want the story that you're telling yourself to continue? Are you even aware of your story?

What thoughts race around your mind?

Are you being kind to yourself, or are you putting yourself down?

You have to do your own work!

Learn to mind your thoughts, or like me, suffer the fate!

THE STORIES THAT WE TELL
Circa 2003

A few long and lonely years go by with work, raising children, and no other men in my life. But, today, I had a very nice surprise when I went to work. An email from Alan, my high school sweetheart, whom I haven't seen or heard from in twenty years. I can't believe it, for over twenty years I've worn a necklace that he'd given me.

I don't know why I wore it for so long. It was just a simple gold chain. The ironic part of it all is that I've just parted with the necklace after a trip to Sicily. My children and I met up with my mother and stepfather who were traveling in Italy. In Sicily we stayed with my stepfather's aunt, a beautiful Sicilian woman in her late sixties, still filled with grief over the death of her husband years before.

We stayed with her for almost a week, and although we couldn't speak the same language, I could feel her: her pain, her sadness, her love. I wasn't prepared for that. I didn't even think about it. I guess I thought it would be all more detached, like staying at a bed and breakfast. Nice people, nice visit, but now it's time for me to leave.

I was so moved by this woman and wanting to give her something of myself I reached up and took off the necklace and gave it to her. She began to cry, and my heart gave out to her even more, and I wished I could do something else for her. So, I gave her a hug, and I looked into her eyes and I knew that she knew that I really cared.

Now I'm home for only a week and I get this email from Alan, who, somehow, even though we live miles apart and nowhere near where we grew up, has heard that I'm divorced. Is it a sign? I've got goosebumps! Is this the reason for all I've been through? Is Alan the ONE for me?

Alan's email says he's separated from his wife, and that he's always loved me. His feelings for me have never changed and he's never stopped thinking about me! He wants to meet and take me away for Valentine's weekend. He's living in Colorado but travels a lot to coach golfers. He says he'll fly out to me in North Carolina, and together we'll fly to Sedona, Arizona for a romantic weekend. I'm so excited!

Alan is the one man I think I can trust, even though, he did kiss another girl in high school, but he tried to make it up to me for many years after. Seems kind of silly now. It was just a kiss in high school, but for me at the time, it was pretty devastating. He broke my heart and I had loved him so much, that I just never could give him a chance of hurting me again. Now, I wish he was the man I had married all those years ago. If I can't trust him, a man who loved me for over twenty years, what man can I trust?

I respond back that I'll always love him too and that yes, let's get together for Valentines. I've agreed to let him come and stay with me while my children are home. I've known him forever, and it will be just one night, but I'm feeling guilty about that. He'll be flying in on the thirteenth.

I arrive at the airport nervous, excited, scared. I think I may be making myself sick. He told me he looks just like he did in high school, and when he sees me, he says I do, too, which is sweet, because he really means that the both of us look good. However, when he gives me this compliment, I can't help but bust out in laughter, thinking that Alan himself thinks he looks just as he did in high school. I think Alan is a little offended at first, but I'm laughing so hard, he can't help but come around.

I mean Alan does look good; tall, lean, muscular, in fact, probably in better shape than in high school, and he still has the most beautiful blue eyes. However, it's apparent that he's one of those men with premature grey hair, and at this point, at forty, he's almost fully grey. His skin has that worn weathered look from being outside all day coaching. You know, sailor skin.

The next day on the fourteenth of February, Valentine's Day, we fly to Sedona. It's beautiful, but I'm still not feeling well. I can't tell if it's my nerves that are acting up again, or if I have the flu or both. We pull up to the bed and breakfast and the owner is waiting for us. Alan has arranged for a couple's massage.

I've always wanted to do that; it seems like the perfect romantic beginning for a couple, but instead because I'm feeling unwell, Alan is settling me into the room. He leaves to let me rest while he goes to pick up some medicine for me. He then heads to a restaurant where he picks up a fabulous meal and a dozen long-stem red roses that he had arranged to be delivered and waiting at our table.

The roses are perfect, and Alan serves me in bed. The food tastes so amazing but I'm only able to eat a little. I'm so grateful to feel the love of a man. It all doesn't seem real. I'm so happy but I'm becoming increasingly more anxious. My stomach tightens. When we finish eating. He announces that he has something else for me and pulls out a white stuffed bear carrying a red heart shaped box.

Inside the box is a gold necklace with a beautiful heart shaped diamond pendant. He says it's to replace the one I gave away. My heart, body and mind are on overload. I've never been treated so well, and I'm thinking of all the preparations that he's made as tears begin to pool in my eyes. I feel so badly, that I feel so, bad.

The next day we take a drive to see the Red Rocks. I'm still not feeling one hundred percent, and I'm not sure how comfortable I feel with him. In some ways it feels like we've never been apart, and yet the thought of physically being with him just doesn't seem right.

Touching him, holding his hand, all seem a little awkward.

Almost as if a physical force is repelling us apart. The detachment doesn't seem to be coming from him, I believe that he wants to be with me, and I know too that I want him. But that may be just coming from a place that I'm horny and I want to have sex.

I can't put my finger on why it doesn't feel perfect. It didn't feel like this in high school. Is it because I haven't had any relationships in so long, and the ones that I have had, didn't work? Am I'm self-protecting, not wanting to give my heart away? Am I having a hard time believing that it's true, because it's too good to be true, that he really wants me, or is it because I think he wants me and therefore something has to be wrong? I mean, God forbid I have a love life, much less a good and easy one.

I'm hoping that as the day goes on, I'll start to settle down and actually want to devour him. But it doesn't happen, my nerves are still on high alert. When we arrive back at the bed and breakfast, with the awkwardness still there, I just let my physical needs take over. Kissing him and touching him as if I were a man, being with a woman for only one night. No feelings, just the satisfaction of sex.

The next day we travel to the Boulders Resort, where he's made reservations for a villa. The place is absolutely incredible. As we walk in, I see a large luxurious bed covered in fine white crisp sheets. A wood burning fire is lit, and music is being piped in all over the room and is set to jazz. The lights are dim, and the volume of music is turned down as if to soften the room.

I walk into the bathroom and am surrounded by beige limestone with soft fluffy white bathrobes hanging on the wall. On the counter are toiletries - soaps, shampoo, and lotions, that look too beautiful to open. It's all so breathtaking. Alan has reached into my mind and pulled out the idea of the perfect fairytale weekend, that I always wanted, and I love him, and I love being with him. So WHY am I not feeling anything with him? Where is he? Where am I? Are either of us even here?

For the remainder of the weekend we continue to have this loving and physically satisfying, but empty sex, and when I arrive home, I still don't know what to feel or if I'm capable of feeling.

———⁓⁓⁓⁓⁓———

Life continues on rather ordinarily for a while, as I renew my odd but typical dating pattern, of seeing the men I'm dating, once a month for several months. Alan has been flying me out to a number of locations and I love it! I'm finally getting to travel. I love going to new places, seeing new things, and having these mini adventures.

It feels great to escape the realities of my life. But most of all I love being with him. It feels like I'm home now. I know no matter what I do, he will love me. And believe that whatever I think or feel or imagine, he will support me. I know this, because he tells me.

I let my mind go further into thoughts of having a life with him. What would it look like? Where would we live? How would my kids feel about moving, and would his kids like me? Sexually, I'm still feeling disconnected, but I'm not thinking of that as I fly off to Texas to see him.

When I arrive, he gives me the biggest bear hug and a kiss. Hmmm... the kiss, still feels a little weird. Which one of us is it? He interrupts my thought process to tell me he needs to meet with a player that he's coaching and asks if I mind going with him to the club.

He starts talking about how great the training facility is, and when we arrive, he gives me a tour. He shows me exercises that he has players do to correct certain tendencies, and a video camera that can stop frame by frame, along with an overlay of the correct swing, to show the student exactly what he or she is doing wrong.

My excitement about the golf facility has worn off. Empty and needing him, I'm only halfway listening to him now as I'd wanted him to be focusing on me. The love of his life, the one he can't live without. I begin to tune out more.

We continue on my tour when we run into some friends of his. When the introductions come to Mitch, who is also a golf coach, he doesn't catch my eye other than he's got the stereotypical look of a golfer - short cropped hair, neatly dressed in a collared shirt under a sleeveless V-neck sweater vest, tan khakis - the works.

Suddenly he grabs my attention when I notice him scowling at me. I'm not sure what's going on. I'm a people pleaser, a do-gooder, everybody likes me. I try not to take it personally, but this is the first time I'm meeting this man. He asks Alan, "Where's your wife?"

Ah, that's it. Evidently, he thinks I'm having an affair with Alan. He clearly doesn't know me, or the situation. I would NEVER be with a married man! Especially after what I've been through. Alan, however, doesn't say anything, and I become so uncomfortable that I just head outside, grab a chair and sit down to read a book that I've brought with me.

It's been hours since I've seen Alan. I'm starting to get really angry, so I finally go in to see where he's been. I find him in an office, and not with a player. "What's going on?" I ask. He looks up at me but not really in my eyes, as he sits behind the desk and says that he has a lot of work to do.

"I really don't want to wait any longer," I say as he's reaching into his pockets. He hands me the keys so I can drive back to the hotel, and he can continue to work. I take the keys and turn and walk away without saying anything else.

Luckily, when I arrive back at the hotel, I remember that I've brought my journal and sit and vent with written words, fuming, as I continue to wait alone. Three hours later, at around 7 P.M., he arrives at the hotel and announces that we're meeting people for dinner. We need to leave.

I'm fuming mad and tell him I don't want to go. Practically shouting I ask, "Why did you have me come here if you had so much work to do?"

"I don't know...," he responds, "I like having you around," then pausing, "I guess I shouldn't ask you to come when I'm working, I'm sorry." "Let's talk more after dinner," he says, while finally looking up at me. "We really need to go." "They're waiting for us."

Reluctantly, I head out the door fearful of meeting his friends and of not having any time alone to play, and now to fight. At dinner I'm more quiet than usual, but after a beer I loosen up a little so that I don't appear rude, realizing that they haven't done anything to me. Alan knowing my unhappiness keeps the night fairly short. In the room he again says he's sorry.

I don't even want to fight or talk about it anymore. We have such little time together. Plus, I have enough things going on in my life. I pretend all is well, I need something to enjoy. Right now, I just want to have sex and go to sleep. Hopefully, next time, things will be better.

I had another one of those out of body experiences this week – like the one that I had at the swim meet years ago. I walked into the office to find Lorelei, you remember the only employee that Keith and I had working in the office with us, and Chuck, a young guy I hired to work in the warehouse where I distribute products from.

They are at the front of the warehouse, in the office that Lorelei and I share and are in a heated argument, both of them claiming the other has stolen money out of the cash deposit that was brought in from the store.

As they each argue, telling their side of the story, I felt as if I literally rose above all of it, like I was really looking down on all of us from above, and I had a deeper knowing, a calm, a peace that seemed to transcend the drama that was going on below. Like all of this didn't really matter in the grand scheme of things.

My ability to stay calm is either from being beaten down so much or may stem from the work I've been doing on myself since the divorce, reading every self-help book possible for the last three years at night and on weekends. What else do you do when you only date someone at best, once a month, and you don't always have your children?

I've read so many self-help books, because when your husband leaves you for someone younger, and before Alan, no one else seemed to want to see you more than a few times, then you seriously start to consider, and then believe, that the problem must be you.

It's been amazing how far I believe I've come. Literally, every three months, I reflect on myself and I'm like wow, look how far I've come. Feeling like I've had a lifetime of growth, but I haven't really figured it all out. Maybe I'm just starting to wake up.

With Chuck and Lorelei, I feel like I've already lost. It didn't matter who took the money. I loved them both, and it really seems silly to me in this moment in the grand scheme of things, of how really insignificant this was, after all I've been through. It's painful though, I mean I've helped them both.

Chuck, his girlfriend and her children lived with me for a few weeks, while they were between housing, and I had given his girlfriend money to renew her Certified Nursing Assistant license. And, for Lorelei, I'd cosigned on an automobile for her, when her parents wouldn't, so that she could buy a car. So maybe it was because I couldn't really believe that either one would steal from me, and as with everything of the last few years. I have too much to deal with, so I let it go.

Maybe I haven't really changed so much.

A few weeks later, my day starts off with my dishwasher breaking. A minor inconvenience, but an inconvenience, nonetheless. Today was already going to be more stressful than normal, as I'm beginning to move my workspace, *again*, this time the contents of my 6000 square feet of warehouse space, which is filled from top to bottom to a larger 10,000 square foot warehouse.

It's a *huge* undertaking itself, *and* it's also Wednesday, our day that we ship out our products to the store. In order for the consumer to save money, our products are back hauled. Meaning that the company that we supply brings a truck on their way back into the warehouse, giving us a set day to get the orders out so that they can be taken to another warehouse to be redistributed.

Because of this, we're always swamped on Wednesdays with last minute orders. The repair of the dishwasher can definitely wait. It's essential that we start packing to move immediately after the orders go out. We need to be up and running no later than next Monday morning in order to be able to fulfill next week's shipment.

Upon arrival at the warehouse, I walk in to find that the bathroom toilets in the office and warehouse have overflowed onto the floor. So instead of filling orders, or billing or packing boxes, I was mopping, plunging and cleaning. Having cleaned the bathrooms, but with no real work being started, the phone rang with an unusual caller.

The man on the other end of the phone said, "Your driver gave me a check for $150,000. I called the bank and they said it wasn't good."

"I don't know what you're talking about," I reply. "I don't have any of my own truck drivers. I would never send any driver with a check, and I wasn't buying anything for a hundred and fifty grand!... Who are you again?"

I ask him to fax me a copy of the check, and it is, in fact, my check and my signature. Someone must have stolen it and somehow washed the check except for my signature, and then reissued it with this man's name on it. I don't understand why or how but I really don't have time for that right now.

I call my bank and explain what has happened. I think they believe I'm crazy, because I'm getting a little frantic and I'm speaking quickly and not clearly. I have so much to do, so I blurt my story out and get off the phone. About an hour later Justin calls from the vitamin store. He tells me the credit card processor isn't working. He's called someone to fix it, but they need the backup CD to reinstall it, and he asks me to bring it by. I've already packed up a few things that I didn't think we would need, and now I have to find it.

I'm wondering how our shipment is going. I look out into the warehouse and Lorelei is handling everything, including all of the invoicing. She says she'll make sure everything gets shipped out. Thank God! I take a deep breath, and start looking for the disc that Justin needs when another strange call comes in. It's a bank in California stating that a couple just came into their branch saying that they've applied for an online loan, and that they received my check in the mail.

They wanted to verify it, which again doesn't make any sense to me. I told them my story of what happened earlier and asked them to also fax me a copy of the check. This time the check was a reproduction and my signature had been forged. *No*, I said, *the check is not good!*

Back on the phone with my bank, I'm feeling more frantic than ever, with thoughts scrambling around in my head about our move, about shipping out, about the awareness of needing to be set up on Monday in order to continue business as usual, all the while knowing that I'm leaving on Friday to go see Alan again, when my personal banker finally answers.

I listen as she tells me that I need to close my account and open a new one. I need to give her a list of checks that have been written and not cleared. So, I get to work on this new assignment that I really have no time for. A few hours later I look up, our shipment has successfully gone out, and my list to the bank has been delivered.

We need to get to work on packing. I start in the office while the rest of the crew works in the warehouse. I find the CD that Justin needs and deliver it later that evening to the store, and as I do, I'm reminded, that they were unable to make charges all day. In the back of my mind I knew that, but I can't think of lost sales now, I have children at home that need to be fed.

The next morning, I head off to work hoping that it'll be a better day than yesterday, I mean it has to be, right? I arrive at the office to get busy, there's a message left on the answering machine, in a southern slang, from the carpet installers. "We ran out of carpet yesterday. We thought we had more in our warehouse, but we don't. We'll have to come back next week to install the carpet on them back two offices."

"Oh yay, now we get to get to set up temporary offices so that we can order and invoice and then we get to take it back down the following week and do it all over again. I love doing things twice and I have so much free time," I say, speaking sarcastically to myself. Last weekend, I spent my time painting the new office. I'm always worn too thin. I take a deeper breath than normal, but literally, I have no time to worry, I need to refocus. I shake my head a little as I take a deep breath in.

Okay, where are we, we should be loading the truck now. The truck, Where's the fucking truck? Now, you know I'm mad because I only cuss when I'm extremely, extremely upset. It's too much. I call the sales rep with the trucking company, and find out he's on vacation, and no one knows anything about a truck coming here.

"Are you fucking kidding me?" I think he hears the crazed panic in my voice because they quickly find a solution. They'll have one of the managers come and drop a trailer off, and then when a driver comes in later, they'll have him come over and deliver it to the new location. I guess that's one advantage of being in the warehouse district. Thank you, I say with sincere appreciation, thank you very much! As I finally allow myself to breathe again.

This delay means that we're even more behind, and I catch myself thinking of Alan, *boy do I need to see him after this week. It'll be nice to feel loved and taken care of, even if just for a little bit.* At this point, a hug would really be nice, but I don't have time to think any more about that. What am I doing? Ah yes, the truck - it's here!

We work late into the night loading, and then go to unload the truck at our new warehouse location. Tomorrow we'll go to work. "All we have to do," I say a little sarcastically to myself, "is set up shelving, organize hundreds of items on the shelves in alphabetical order, set up temporary offices and computer locations for billing, and then whatever isn't finished will have to wait for Lorelei on Saturday. It's late and we all need to go home."

My children are with their father tonight. I head straight to bed. Friday comes and we accomplish a lot before I head to the airport. Lorelei has her hands full, but she can handle it, she's amazing. I don't know what I would've done the last few years without her, and I'm thinking many grateful thoughts as I fly off.

I arrive in Texas, and make my way to baggage claim, where I see Alan waiting for me. Thank God! I give him the biggest hug I believe I've ever given anybody. I just want to melt and let him take care of me. He has no idea whatsoever what's been going on in my life. We haven't had time to talk.

Alan is working with some players this weekend, but I'm excited to see him, and to be away from the madness. Something is strange though, he seems more distant and distracted than usual, as we drive to the hotel. I wonder what's on his mind. I want so much to tell him about my week, and at the same time I don't really want to relive it. So instead, I wait until we get to the hotel and I tell him a watered-down version.

I'm really confused, and I have to say I was very disappointed in his response, even if I did tell him a glossed-over version. I expected something. Some kind of reaction, but the response I got was more of the response you get when you tell someone what you've ordered for lunch that day. Like, "Oh, really Hmm…," as he looks away, and then turns and walks away, ending with his back to me as he stares out the window.

"What's going on?" I ask.

"I'm thinking it might be too soon for us," he says. I stiffen.

"I'm just not ready."

"What are you saying," I ask, not believing what I'm hearing.

"I have some things to work out on my own. With the family, the kids, the divorce, and I think I need to deal with some old issues that I haven't dealt with."

I've been standing and I slowly sink down to the edge of the bed, thinking I may fall, numb, not knowing what to say, and not saying anything. I sit like this for a very long time. I don't know what Alan is doing. I'm in my own little world of blankness. After what seems like moments but was probably hours, I lay down in bed with my back to him, immobile and still, but with eyes wide open. I lay in this zombie-like state until I fall asleep.

The next morning I'm still emotionless. I'm going through the movements but I'm not exactly sure how. I think I'm in a state of shock, playing nice again, as if nothing happened. This seems to be my default reaction after my conditioning with Keith, and the only way I know how to handle this blow.

Alan, didn't really end things with me, did he? Not him, not this, and not after this week. Of all the men, I thought he was the one I could trust with my heart. If a man who said he loved me for twenty years, doesn't love me, then who will?

I'm finished packing and still in this state of shock as we begin to head down the hall to our continental breakfast together in the Comfort Inn lobby. It's nice, but it's a far cry from where we started in the luxurious surroundings in Sedona, with his words of praise and love. To the now generic surroundings of commercial grade carpet, and wood grained plastic laminate tables, without barely a glance in my direction. Which just makes this ending worse or fitting. We speak only a few words as he runs off to work with a student. I call a cab and fly home. Robotically, I keep moving.

Monday morning is a new day at the office. I arrived first. Lorelei is amazing. The warehouse is set up with rows of shelves, products are neatly stacked on top of them, with labels, neatly marked with product codes and items in alphabetical order. The office itself is still in disarray, but we can ship, and I should be able to set something up today, so that we can bill.

Lorelei arrives in a panic. Her soon to be ex-husband has resurfaced over the weekend and has apparently been threatening her. She talks for fifteen minutes, non-stop, giving me the full details. Feeding off her energy, I become more and more tense, and I really don't think I can handle any more, I may burst. I'm panicking now.

Lorelei sensing this says, "Don't worry, I've taken a restraining order out on him." "Lorelei, Ned is crazy!" I say almost screaming, from the accumulated stress. "He scares me! He always has!"

I feel at this point that I want to crawl out of my own skin. Ned is the type of man that when you walk into the room you feel his presence. You feel yourself tightening, and tensing your muscles, even when he's being polite. You're uncomfortable and you don't want him near you, you just want to get far, far, away. It doesn't help that I've heard of his abuse from Lorelei for a very long time. And, I fear the image I have, imaginary or not, of him running into the office with a gun. I didn't need to hear more.

My first thought was that I can't handle any of this. I can't deal with this too. Lorelei had been a champion for me, but the best I can do right now, for both of us is to send her home, with a paid week off. However, that leaves me doing both of our jobs. I'm not sure I can handle that either, after the last few days, and really years, come to think of it. But I believe it's better than this fearful energy that I keep feeling. I'm so on the edge right now, I'm afraid it might just throw me over. The day marches on and so do I.

On the way home I stop at the convenience store to pick up some milk, it's raining a little, and as always, I'm in a hurry to get home to Max and Ally. I open up the car door and take two steps, when kid you not, the sky opens up and dumps a bucket full of water on me. I only literally had five steps to make, and when I step into the store, I'm completely soaking wet. What the hell is going on? What have I done to deserve all of this? Am I not going to get any slack?

Tuesday morning, we have our weekly sales meeting. Justin, Quinn, and Jonathan are here from the vitamin store. I want to be brief because I have so much work to do, but it's come to my attention that they're ordering products that we carry in our warehouse from another vendor.

Which is one of the main reasons I opened the store - increased sales, and inventory reduction. Apparently, the other vendor sells it cheaper to them than I do. I remind them that money stays in the same place, because we're the same company, and ordering from our warehouse makes us stronger as a whole.

They don't seem to be getting what I'm saying, they are only thinking of the store's bottom line. I must not be explaining myself to them well. I'm overcome, and in exasperation, I look up to the sky and say with a vengeance and with a disbelief of all that has happened in the past week, "Okay God,... Give it to me, I can handle it, I'm still standing!"

And, the room instantly becomes eerily silent and still. I immediately begin to have a sick feeling, but it's too late, it's already been said. I let everyone go, and quickly begin racing around the office, checking in freight, invoicing, answering the phone. I'm exhausted and I need to leave early to get my daughter, she has soccer practice tonight.

I rush home, pick up my daughter, and speed off to practice. We're only going to be a few minutes late when the truck in front of me stops short. I slam on my brakes, but I'm too close and going too fast. We slam into the truck. I look back at Ally, we're both visibly shaken but okay.

Thank God I didn't let her sit up front like she had wanted. The front passenger side window now has a two-by-four sticking through it. I can't move. I mean I physically can, but I'm so shaken up that I can't. A woman rushes to the door.

"Are you okay?"

"Yes, yes..., are the people in the truck okay?"

"Yes," she says, "but the man on the passenger side is complaining about his neck. We called the ambulance."

"Thank you," I mumbled. Then feeling even more guilty and ashamed that my mind wanders to the fact that I just wrecked my brand-new SUV. One payment down, fifty-nine more to go. I'm sorry God, you win, I can't handle any more.

Wednesday arrives and it's our day to ship out again, and as usual we have several last-minute orders come in to be filled and billed. It's a normal weekly stress but much harder without Lorelei, but we pull it off.

I think I'll let Lorelei catch up on the rest of her work when she gets back. I need to focus on my own. Yay! The day is over, and Thursday and Friday come and go without a hitch. Happy for the end of the week. Next week has got to be better.

I head home. Max and Ally are playing at Richard and Emma's house, so I stop by. It's really been a blessing for my children and me, that when my friends moved back from Austria, they bought a home just down the street from us. It's like a third home for the children, and I have the peace of mind that someone is nearby watching over them.

They also happen to be the only couple that still invites me over. Seems that when you get divorced you lose not only your children part of the time, your husband, his family, but your friends and your way of living. I love Richard and Emma both individually and even more as a couple. They give me hope that love with someone is possible, and that good men really do exist.

Richard is Venezuelan, and naturally affectionate, which makes me uncomfortable for some reason. Not because I think he would hit on me; he would never do that. It may be that I'm just not used to anyone hugging me. I see Ally, acting just like me. I think it makes Richard hug us more. I think he's trying to loosen us up.

Emma is fabulous in her own right and has this beautiful essence of confidence and self-respect. She has a profound wisdom and insight, which you would think one would only get after living a long hard life with deep introspection. We are the same age, though, and I can barely understand what's going on around me at this point.

With her three children, she's the glue that keeps everyone together. Emma, always the generous host is not any different today as she invites me into her home and heart and pours me a glass of wine. She says, "I need to tell you something." As she pauses for just a moment. "Ally has been crying all day," pausing again, "Keith is getting married."

I sink into the chair and feel as if someone has punched me in the gut for the 9000th time this week. Is she kidding? My thoughts race. Ally never cries, I often worry at how tough she is, and how she holds all her emotions in. How did her father tell her? I thought she liked Kimberly. And of course, he tells the kids before telling me.

It would have been helpful for the children's sake for me to be prepared. I knew this would happen one day. Heck, they've been together eight years now. Four years while we were married, and four years afterward, I don't know why they've waited. But this really sucks hearing it from my friend and not Keith.

Unfortunately, since the divorce I still talk to him on a daily basis, as we coordinate the children's activities, which continues to feel like my daily gut punch. Coward - why didn't he tell me? It would have been nice to be prepared for this.

My mind begins to wander into self-defeating chatter. Why can't I have a good life? Why don't things ever work out for me? What's wrong with me? I try to talk to Ally, but she's not opening up to me. I don't know how to talk to her or maybe anyone for that matter. I'm not sure what to do, as the "poor me" mind chatter continues on into the night.

Saturday morning, we have a team soccer meeting at one of the parent's homes. Keith is there of course. Now that we're divorced, he's freaking dad of the year. Attending all the soccer games, parent teacher conferences, and even doctors' appointments.

Now he's available all the time for everything. It feels as if he's haunting me, shadowing me, and pestering me like a mosquito that won't go away. After the meeting, I confront him outside about how he told the kids the news about his engagement.

We have a big blow out in front of many parents, and a few children. Not my proudest moment, but I needed to vent, and he was a target I didn't mind hitting. F.U. Keith, F.U. Alan, F.U. truck rep, F.U. identity thieves, but not you God, I say fearing more retribution. I *love* you!

A week later I wish I could say things are getting better, besides the normal stresses of work and being a single mother. I'm still trying to handle some of the underlying currents of the recent events. My dishwasher can't be fixed and needs to be replaced, so two plus unproductive days dealing with the smallest of my troubles.

And, I'm feeling bad about being aggravated about that, because today I received a letter with my $150,000-dollar check. It was from the man who first alerted me to the theft of checks, when he asked about the check given to him from the driver of a truck. I had forgotten that I'd asked him to send it to me, and in the letter, he apologizes for the delay. He, as a result of this experience, had to spend a few days in the hospital. Something to do with his heart, he didn't elaborate.

My heart too hasn't stopped hurting. Who knows how many days or weeks, or months or years it'll take to fix? I still feel blank. Maybe it's because I don't have time to deal with it, and maybe it's because I have to keep moving forward. I feel as if I have no choice. Too many people are depending on me.

I always carry this feeling with me of the weight and burden of how many people and families that are affected by my decisions, or lack of them, and the number of people and families that would suffer. I have to keep moving forward, but these continual blows are making it so much harder. Nine thousand dollars damage on my new SUV, and the injured man may sue. Thank God, none of us were injured more.

With perfect timing, Brian the guy I met at the corporate banquet years ago, sent me an email today out of the blue. It's really been a long time since I've heard from him. He's writing about his struggles.

His fiancé, who he stopped seeing me for, left him. You know the one who just wanted to breathe him in, she's now seeing his friend. His store is not doing well. He continues on and on, and ends with, "Why do things go right for you and not me?"

I froze, I can't believe I just read that last sentence. My emotions are all still so fresh and raw after these last two weeks, that I can't believe I'm still standing. So, after a very deep breath, and no energy to reply, I simply hit delete. Yes, my life is so effing perfect.

On one small but positive note, we're finally set up from our move, in our newly carpeted offices, and we're organized. However, some of our products have not shipped from our vendors. Apparently, the bank has stopped payment on some of the checks they should have let through.

The manufacturers are questioning my story about identity theft. It all seems a little fishy to them, coupled by an address change. They want to know what's really going on. It seems they're willing to wait for the new checks to arrive and clear before shipping. Now the stores I supply are wondering why they can't get all the products this week. Yup - my life is fucking perfect!

The following week my bank statement arrives and evidently Miller, one of my warehouse employees, has stolen two checks, and it's on my new account! The fool has written them to himself, and I wonder if somehow, he's related to the other missing checks.

How could Miller be so stupid. He's only eighteen but, come-on. Only two months ago, I gave him money to buy tires. I call the bank again, and they don't seem to believe that I now have something wrong with this new account. It looks like I'm going to have to eat this loss. I report it to the police, but other than that I don't have the strength or energy to fight. He's disappeared, and I notice a computer is missing too. I wonder what else is missing from the move. F.U. Brian, and F.U. Miller.

THE STORIES THAT WE TELL
Circa 2003

I'm turning forty, so I'm keeping my promise of traveling even if I'm alone. I need a break and something happy to look forward to, so a few days ago, I flew into London, then caught a plane to Istanbul where I'm staying for two nights. I researched the culture a little bit before I traveled. It's so much different from any place that I've ever been before, which I guess, is the point of why I'm here.

As I head to the markets, I see large baskets filled with spices that are so beautiful and fragrant. The streets are truly a mixture of east meeting west, in clothing and in the modernization of this ancient city by the many electrical wires that run next to the street.

In the distance, I hear the beautiful melodic sounds of mosque calling people to prayer. Everyone I meet seem really nice and kind. They keep wanting to know where I'm from, and surprisingly they keep guessing that I'm from Israel. I'm staying at a Hotel near the airport. I visit the Hagia Sofia. It's hard to believe that it's fifteen hundred years old, it's so large, so beautiful, so majestic.

I found out that it's spent the first thousand years of its life as an Eastern Orthodox Cathedral, then for a few years as a Roman Catholic Cathedral before being converted in the 1400's to an Ottoman Mosque before it's conversion to a museum in the 1930's. Bringing to my awareness of how objects, like people and nations, have their stories. Tomorrow I'm taking a plane to Kusadasi, a seaside resort next to the Aegean Sea.

I underestimated how it would feel flying on a Turkish airline not speaking the language. It's been a little bit more challenging than I thought, finding only one person who spoke a little English to help me navigate around the airport upon arrival. I take a ride to the resort where I'm staying and feel grateful to have arrived.

The place is beautiful, and the prices are really reasonable. I feel as if I can finally let myself set up all the things that I would normally restrict myself from due to cost. I sign up for a day trip to a Greek Island. I schedule a massage, a few hours to scuba dive, and set up a meeting with a travel agent.

I'm traveling down the coast in a few days to Bodrum, to a place where individuals traveling solo can meet up. I've chosen the option of sharing a room with another solo traveler. I can't wait, it's supposed to be a really cool Bohemian type of vibe.

Today I walk outside and ask the cab driver to drive me around so that I can see the sites. He takes me first to a place to buy rugs. It was not what I was thinking, I was envisioning seeing the town and sights. I don't think either of us really understands each other, but I'm here so why not. I get out of the car, and I go about my own business looking around.

I see a woman making a rug on what appears to be a large loom. Hand threading from what looks like naturally colored fibers. I walk back outside to another building, when at the same time I feel a presence behind me, I hear a man's voice in English, say, "May I help you?"

I answer back, "I don't know, can you?" I smile as I turn around, surprised to meet an English speaker here.

He introduces himself as Ahmet, the boss of this establishment, he gives me a tour and tells me all about the history of the rugs of Turkey going back centuries. He shows me many rugs but an Oushak rug that was made in nearby Uşak, Turkey, is speaking to me. I had no intention of buying a rug, but it's incredibly beautiful, and authentic, and real, that I want one.

I tell him I would like one for a large room. He says he has more, and he'll have someone bring them by boat, from where exactly, I don't know. He offers me some tea while I wait for the new samples to arrive, which I greatly appreciate. I meander through all the out-buildings and an hour later he summons me to the main building where the new rugs have just been brought in.

They are made in a nearby village, where I'm told the weavers' techniques have been passed down through generations, father to son, mother to daughter. The fibers are all-natural vegetable dye, and the one that I'm drawn to me is made out of cotton and wool. The background is a golden ivory color, with large floral motifs of red and light green. I pay and he says he'll have it shipped to me.

He tells me that he sends them all over the world and has just come back from a trip from New York where he brought several rugs for people to try them out in their homes. He says I got a really good deal because he sells them in New York for ten to twenty thousand for the same size rug. I thank him. He asks if I want to meet him for dinner. I smile and say yes, but my stomach is acting up again. I'm starting not to feel well. We agree to meet in two hours.

I head back to the hotel and lay down for a bit. In Turkey the electricity in the whole hotel is turned off for a few hours each day to save energy, and it's pretty warm in my room, but it is a great way to get people outside and enjoying life.

At dinner I arrive to find Ahmet with someone he introduces to me as his boss. I'm grateful that he too speaks English. Ahmet says it wouldn't have been proper for us to meet alone. I learn a lot about the Turkish culture that night. For instance, when you buy real estate you meet-up with the property owner and you arrive with the funds.

The property is then transferred into your name, and it becomes yours just like that; no waiting, no reams of papers, but also no loans. He orders Raki for the table, the unofficial Turkish drink, similar to Greeks Ouzo. It's a clear liquid and he pours a little water in it making it milky white. I take a sip, but I tell him that I'm really not feeling well.

He asks if I want to see a doctor. And I say that I think I do; he picks up his phone and calls a friend of his. He pays the bill and takes me to the doctor's office. It's after hours, but the doctor meets us at his office. After a few questions and examination, he gives me a prescription to get filled. I thank him and he doesn't let me pay him, as he said he's here for Ahmet.

Ahmet drives me back to the hotel. The next day, I go downstairs to catch a ride to find out where to get my prescription filled. I must look really bad, and I feel hot and clammy. I tell the driver what I need to do before getting into the car. He tells me he will go get it for me and bring it back to the hotel.

The other employees nearby let me know it's a normal thing to do. I go back to my room and moments later my prescription arrives. Ahmet calls to check in on me. I'm not able to keep any food down. He calls the hotel and makes special arrangements for them to serve me boiled potatoes all week. The hotel is all inclusive. I'm a little disappointed to not be able to eat all of the delicious food I see, and I can't go on my prepaid adventure to the Greek Island that's leaving right now. But, I'm so grateful to have met Ahmet. It feels nice to have someone looking out for you.

For the rest of the week I make do, trying to get out of the room during the day because of the heat and lack of air conditioning. I'm meeting a lot of people, which seems like it's easier to do when traveling alone. One woman who looked to me to be about 65 and also traveling alone, told me that she had been all over the world and she always travelled alone and always meets the best people. It was inspiring, but it also made me a little sad. I didn't want to be traveling all alone for the rest of my life.

Today, I'm supposed to be leaving for my prepaid trip to Bodrum. But, I'm 100% sure I'm not able to travel right now, as I keep having trouble keeping food down. So, I keep spending my days at the hotel eating potatoes, but it's not all bad I have to say. Since, there's no electricity inside during the day. I sit under the shade of the umbrella next to the pool, which is also next to the Aegean Sea. It's a breathtaking site, and the sound of the sea is soothing.

The hotel checks on me a few days later. I'm grateful and surprised. I'm not used to anyone, much less a hotel staff, even being aware of me, much less to check in on me. I'm usually the one taking care of everyone. I must look worse than I believe. It's been a week since I've seen Ahmet's doctor. The hotel offers to have another doctor come to my room, and I graciously accept.

I tell the doctor that I've had trouble for years with my stomach, but I think I might have eaten something that didn't agree with me. I confessed to eating something from a street vendor in Istanbul. He says yes, it might be something my body just isn't used to. He's very kind and has a very gentle manner about him. He says he'll have some medicine sent up to my room, and he charges me a very small fee for the visit.

A few days later the travel agent that I had scheduled all my trips with comes to my room. She's in her twenties, beautiful, kind and caring. She apologizes for not being able to refund the excursions but helps me change all my returning flights that I've missed and suggests that I go with her tomorrow on a little outing through town. I'm feeling a little better and think it will be fun. I love seeing how people really live, and I feel a connection to her.

The next day, Zel, my travel agent, picks me up outside the hotel. We drive to a nearby village and get out of the car. We walk through the streets, and through people's yards. She grabs a fruit off a tree and begins to eat it. I follow her into someone's home. The house is small, like most of them appear to be.

The windows are open, and the breeze blows through. Zel speaks to the women in the home in Turkish, and then continues to show me around the house. It's clean and neat, but very, very minimal. The walls are a shade of old white linen. The L-shape sofa lines two sides of the house, it's attached to the walls made from the same type of clay plaster.

There are no cushions, pillows, fabric, or color in this room. No paintings inside, just a single framed picture of what appears to be a family member. I ask Zel if she knows the woman. "No" she says. "In our culture if anyone comes to your door, you welcome them."

I smile at the homeowner as we leave, to thank her, hoping she feels what's coming from my heart. We leave and go to a cafe type place nearby. Zel asks if I've ever had ayran.

"No, I haven't, what is it?"

"It's a Turkish drink made out of yogurt."

"I'm sorry," I say, "I haven't had anything other than potatoes to eat for over a week, I'm afraid to try it, Besides I don't like yogurt."

And, then she waves her arm as if to say nonsense "It will be good for your stomach, you will see."

The beverages arrive, and not wanting to insult, I drink, while fearing what it will do to my stomach. A moment later she gets up and says, "Let's walk to the old building." When we arrive, we walked into what appears to be an old church, in an ancient city called Ephesus.

It also looks like it's been as a mosque and now it's looks to have been abandoned for decades. It's small, and the windows are missing, and so is part of the roof. It looks centuries old, and beautiful paintings of Christ and Madonna and child are being revealed as the weather wears away later updates. The paintings look like they should be in a museum. There's a real essence to this place and the people here. I feel very grounded, centered, happy and safe.

We head out to see more sights, pose for some pictures and later sit down for a cup of Turkish tea. I really feel like I'm pushing it today. It's my first day out, and my second glass of something other than water, but Zel really wants to read my tea leaves. She looks at them and then at me. Then says, "I want to tell you a story that my mother has told me."

Taking a deep breath in, she starts, "As we go through life we may run into people and situations that we've already been in. Why do you want to keep repeating it, going over and over it in your head? When a relationship is over, why do you want to keep reliving it? If you read a book cover to cover, why do you need to pick it back up? You know what it says, you know how it ends. Close the book and put it away."

I head back to the hotel in a bit of a dazed silence. How can this beautiful young woman, who is half my age, know so much about me? And how did she know that the tea and the yogurt drink wouldn't upset my stomach? I am feeling a little better physically.

Later Ahmet checks in on me by phone. I tell him I'm worried, I'm out of money, and have been having trouble using my credit card. He says he'll send a driver to take me to the bank. He'll help me get it straightened out.

The driver arrives and takes me to the bank. I'm a little concerned because he doesn't seem to speak any English. He motions to me what I believe means give the teller my credit card, words are said, and I leave with my card working and money to spend. It works out perfectly. Tomorrow I fly back to Istanbul and then the next day to London. The people of Turkey have been amazing to me. I've been treated with kindness and respect, and, I've become a little bit of a celebrity of the hotel. I've been here so long that the staff all seem to know me, and my potatoes. All support is appreciated.

The next day I take myself to get the massage that I paid for so long ago. I'm worried, however, that I'm just going to spread whatever it is inside me that's making me sick. I'm supposed to be on vacation, and I hate that it's the first time where I've allowed myself to spare no expense, that I'm not getting to enjoy any of it, so I'm going!

I arrive to find a larger than expected room covered in beautiful blue and green tiles, with dimmed soft light and gentle music playing. I lay down on warm marble and as the massage barely begins, a single tear rolls out of the corner of my eye.

I don't want to go home. I take care of everyone, and I'm finding that I like people looking after me, even if it's just a little bit. It's been really rough being sick, laying around day after day alone, but I've had so many wonderful people taking care of me, without even asking. Maybe that's why I don't want to go home. Just a few kind simple gestures, is all it takes. But I'm already a week past the date I should have returned, and people are worried about me being alone and sick in a foreign country.

After the massage, I stroll down to the sea to a place where I can be alone. It's not hard to do, the wind is really blowing forcefully, and not many people are out. I find a spot on a dock right next to the sea. The wind is blowing in huge gusts, and the waves keep splashing up on me. I can see the mountains and the Greek islands in the distance. Two birds fly by as waves continue to crash on the rocks. The spray hits my whole body and it makes me laugh. It's warm outside.

I lay on my stomach and think, yes, I need to close this book. I know how it ends: unhappily. I need to start anew.

Heading home from Turkey I arrive in London, I'm still not feeling very well, and I'm feeling a little sorry myself and my "spoiled" vacation. I check myself into the five-star Mandarin Oriental Hotel - Hyde Park. Why not? It's only going to be one night. I walk into the room, and it's breathtaking. Champagne is on ice, and the room overlooks a street with lots of glittery shops. People are busy and moving. This place feels alive.

Piped into the room is a radio station playing classical music. I decide to take a bath. I pop open the champagne and pour it into a sparkling crystal glass. I take it into the bathroom and step into warm bubbly suds. I take a deep breath and then a sip of my champagne. I don't really even like champagne, but at this moment it's making me feel very special, so I'm going to sip on it some more.

As I soak, I begin to look around at the white marble that's everywhere. An antique cherry vanity that's been stained dark is to my right, and the contrast of light marble and dark wood is breathtaking. Next to that is a water closet and bidet. Above the wall is painted two shades of off white, separated by wood molding framing tasteful artwork.

Under the window is a beautiful chrome plated towel warmer with the most luxurious big white fluffy towels. Next to them lay white linen hand towels perfectly pressed. The shower is also all white marble, as is the tub next to it. I'm staring at the reflections of the water in the chrome faucet, just allowing myself to get lost in time, as the waves from my subtle movement send prisms of light all around the room.

I feel in this moment a sense beyond satisfaction, and at the same time have the thought that if I were to die, it would be okay, because I would have had this perfect moment. Then, as if reading my thoughts, the radio broadcaster asks the question: *"If you were to write an essay, describe what you would do if you had one day to change your life."*

I pause taking in this question. I don't know where to begin, but simply recognize further how very lucky I am to be able to even have this moment. I take a deep breath and allow myself to truly savor it. And, as if soaking in the tub, also soaked in all of these really good feelings.

I am starting to feel like a very lucky girl. I begin thinking, this may be the only time I'm ever in London. So, I need to get up and put on that cute cocktail dress that I've brought with me but haven't worn and go out and meet some people. But when I get to the closet, my bravery has already waned a bit, and I reach for a nice pair of pants and shirt instead, that makes me feel more conservative, but also stylish and classy.

I walk down the hall toward the hotel restaurant located on the lower level, and as I get closer, I noticed a bar straight ahead. It looks really happening. I glance to the right to see   the restaurant almost empty. Maybe I'm too early. I decide I would feel more comfortable at the bar than eating alone in an empty restaurant and head in.

Everyone here seems busy and preoccupied. I've noticed over the last few years, when I've taken myself out to eat, that there is no need to worry about being alone at a restaurant. People seem to only focus on themselves, and who they're with, barely looking up to those around them.

I think, however, that this is a bar and not a restaurant, and that people may be looking, I feel a little less comfortable, but I make my way into the bar, looking for a seat when a man stands up and offers his to me. He says he's leaving for dinner soon, but then lingers. A man across the bar sends me a drink, and a couple of loud men come and sit next to me. The man closest to me with dark hair starts chatting with me. He has a really great personality and is really fun to talk to. Until he starts leaning in, invading my personal space. He gets uncomfortably close.

Luckily, he has to go meet a friend. He tries to convince me to go with him, but I decline. At the exact time that he finally leaves, a man walks ups to me and introduces himself as Daniel. I, with large eyes say, "What took you so long?" Feeling a little like I may have needed to be rescued. He asks if I want to join him and his friend at their table. I agree and head over. He then introduces me to, I kid you not, Allen.

Not "the" Allen, or "the" Daniel, but Yup Daniel and Allen, the names of the two men my heart really felt something for. Another reminder of unrequited love, and of being alone. How am I ever going to close this book? I excuse myself and head to my room.

As I arrive back home, I'm immediately thrust back into my life, as if I had never left. Forgetting any lessons that I had learned, and for the next few years my head, my heart and my life stayed down in the trenches. More toasts alone at New Years. More work, more of trying to be the best mom I could possibly be. More preparations for a secure future. More heart wrenching struggles along the way.

THE STORIES THAT WE TELL
Circa 2005

Justin, who runs my vitamin store, fiancé left him out of the blue. After a typical morning spent with her; eating breakfast together, making plans for the evening, etc. He came home from work at the end of the evening to find her engagement ring on his kitchen counter.

I'm so impressed with how well he's handling it; his resiliency is inspiring. Just a few months later he's on a dating website. He says, he's ordering his perfect girl – "Look here," he says, as I peer over his shoulder to the computer at the store. Excitedly he says, "I can put in exactly how I want my girl to look, curvy, tall, whatever, then it shows me all the women that meet that criteria."

He's on a Christian site, he says, "I just want a nice girl. She doesn't have to have any money or anything. She can even drive an old blue Subaru like me, and I wouldn't care." And, sure enough, in just a few weeks he meets a beautiful Brazilian girl who lives in New Jersey. Her family has one car. It's an old blue Subaru, just like his. They are really hitting it off. I'm so inspired that I take to the internet like a storm.

I log onto multiple sites looking for Mr. Right. I find someone I think I would like to go out with. He seems super nice, but apparently, he lied on his information. He said he was tall, one of the criteria I selected. You know picking out what you want. So, me and my naturally 5'8" body show up in very high heels.

I tried to walk around town and spend some time with him, but I feel uncomfortable since I'm not only hovering more than six inches above him, but because I'm wondering why he lied. I might have liked him just as he was if he hadn't lied, but I kind of have this zero-tolerance kind of thing now with men not being honest.

So, I ask, and he answers me by saying "Doesn't everybody lie on these sites." Which makes me uncomfortable not just by what he said, but by how he said it. So, I end the date short, pun intended.

The second guy I went on a date with, I met for dinner. He was attractive and seemed nice, and I have no other explanation as to why it didn't work other than to say - sometimes when you see two good looking people in the gender that you're attracted too, and before they even say a word, as if in some unspoken language, you can be attracted to one of them and not the other. This is what I think happened here.

The third guy and I hit it off right away. He seems really nice and we have a lot of fun. He makes me laugh and I really enjoy spending time with him. We try to date, but I believe he's hung up on the fact that I'm five years older than him. His name is John, he's a builder and we become friends.

I'm still feeling like I'm being punched in the gut every time I talk to Keith, which is daily. It's been too many years of sitting near Keith at soccer games etc. while I continue to be alone. I have the children coming home to my house every day after school so that they don't have to wonder which house they are supposed to go.

But on the days when Keith is supposed to pick the children up, there're no boundaries to the intrusion. He comes into my house to change his clothes on the days he's picking up the kids after work. He always has an excuse, and somehow, it's twisted around and I'm the ridiculous one for not wanting him to use my bathroom and invade my space.

He says, "What, their dad can't come into the house?" "What, I just need to use the bathroom." "What, I just need to change my clothes." These things I believe wouldn't happen, if I had a man in my life.

Later, I try this dating thing one more time. I have this huge hole in me, which was recently confirmed to me while at a health event that our vitamin store was sponsoring. Near our booth, chair massages were being given. The boys, which is what I call Justin and the other guys running my store, suggested I go over and get a massage, and, in a lull I did.

I was getting fully relaxed in the chair ready to receive the chair massage, when all of a sudden, the masseuse touched me on my back and it sent a jolt right through me, this awareness of touch. How long has it been - *since - I've - been - touched*? I guess in my continual state of being busy I hadn't realized how long it had been since someone had touched me, until this jolt went through me. I think I may cry, so I quickly stand back up.

It would be nice if someone would take care of me, if even just for a moment. I've been taking care of everyone for what seems like eternity. A dinner out would be great. I would even be happy if someone made me a cup of coffee, and it would be even better if it was one, I didn't have to pay for.

Anyway, as I said, I'm trying this dating thing again and my date shows up in white tennis shoes, I know it sounds petty but for some reason, after all this time I didn't think my knight in shining armor would be wearing white tennis shoes, and really goes back to what I said about guy number two, that I can't really pinpoint what doesn't work with this guy.

I just know that it doesn't. So, I tell this story like this maybe just for effect or to keep the story short, which makes me realize and come to a conclusion that I'm never going to meet anyone this way. I don't have the time or patience for any of it.

John, my builder friend, who I also met from this dating website, is down the street, so I used him as my excuse to end the date. I just don't think it's going to work for me like this, but I pat myself on the back for at least trying. In the back of my mind I wonder if part of it was because I know John is around the corner. I have so much fun with him, that I just don't want to waste my time, because I would rather spend time with him.

My relationship with John moved a long time ago more into the state of brother - sister, and I'll take that right now. I don't have any family nearby, except of course my beautiful children who I'm not discounting, but they are not old enough yet to help me out of any situation, and they don't know how to make coffee. So, it's nice to finally have someone to call in case of an emergency.

John and I promise each other that if we ever end up old and alone, we'll buy houses side by side and keep each other company on the front porch, and as crazy as that sounds, it gives me a little comfort.

On the business front, as soon as I begin hearing word that I may lose the distribution end of my business, it happens. I knew it wouldn't be forever, it's just the nature of this business, but it doesn't feel good. Especially since it's not because of anything that my company did wrong, but it's more about who knows who. It's eighty percent of my business. I don't have much time to figure it all out, but I do my best to protect all my employees. And, try to figure out what I want to do myself.

My company has a contract with Coca-Cola, doing set work at a grocery store chain. It would be a good salary for me, but I'd have to travel, and I can't do that as a single parent. It's a good opportunity to protect James who's my only salesman right now, and the one who's actually been doing the work. I transfer that opportunity to him and sell him the home and garden products that I also warehouse so that he can continue on with that as well. Together they will pay his salary and expenses.

It was never anything I wanted to do anyway. It was all Keith's dream; helping him and our family. Then it became about opportunity and keeping my family fed, and about doing a good job and continuing the path that I was on. For so long it's been just me and a few employees and whatever truck drivers that have come this way. Which is another reason why I opened up the vitamin store. It was another way for me to be with people.

I need to do something different anyway. I've just felt isolated and alone for so long, first alone in my marriage, which now that I think of it is actually worse than being alone now. Anyway, without any income, I should probably sell my home. I've been buying and selling homes myself for the last few years, in addition to running my business.

I've been making the same, if not more money as my yearly salary. I use my design degree. It's fun except for the moving part and I'm sure the kids don't like that part either. I think maybe it could be fun to get into real estate. At least I would be meeting people.

I live in a desirable neighborhood, the same neighborhood that Keith and I built that house before our separation. The house sells fast, and I begin the search for my new home. This time I believe I should buy a smaller house that I can pay off instead of the larger homes I've been taking a risk with. I really feel that I need a rest and a break. I've asked John to come and take a look at one with me, since he's a builder, and it needs some work. My mom comes too, she's in town visiting.

I love this cute little cottage that I've found but it's really close to where Keith works and I'm not sure I want him driving by all the time, but it sure would be nice to not have to worry about anything for a while. Just focus on me and getting my breath back, maybe even have a social life. My mom gets mad at me as I tell her this. She says, I'm giving up. And, I do, I really want to give up for a while.

I'm so very tired, I haven't felt rested since Max was born, and that was fifteen years ago. A break would be nice, but reluctantly with my head down, I buy a home that's just slightly less expensive than the home I just sold. It's also located in my current neighborhood. It has an unfinished basement, so I know after finishing it, I'll be able to make some money from it.

However, I do make a compromise with myself after moving, I'm going to take Max and Ally, and head to Miami Beach for a month, instead of working at the store. I want them to have a little taste of how I grew up, with the beach and the sand. I don't think I can keep going if I don't. When I get back, I'm going to become a Realtor.

The kids and I have unfortunately or fortunately have become really good at moving, even at their young age. Ally is great at helping me pack and Max is strong and is always good about recruiting friends to help. I just want to be still for a while, I need a break, but no time for that.

Maybe it's being busy that's been keeping me sane. Then I don't have to think about anything other than what task is next. Leaving all emotions out. But right now, it doesn't feel that way. My gut, this internal nudge from within, is telling me to stop. It's just like that feeling I had when I got divorced, telling me to leave the Carolinas. And, it would be nice to one day have a home, and not just a house.

John comes over to look at the basement in my new large home. In the past, I've always remodeled before moving in, so that not only can I enjoy the remodel, but so that it's ready when I need to sell. I usually have it coordinated to begin the remodel as soon as I close on the house. Contractors are ready to come in and work, and all items are purchased and ready to be installed. This is the first time John will be doing anything for me and the first time I'm living in the remodel.

Since it's the basement, I don't expect it to be too bad, and John assures me that I'm correct. I draw up what I would like the remodel to look like and I take it to the city for approval and get all necessary permits. I'm also finishing up my real estate license course and taking the test soon. Since I've been doing this for years now, I thought it would be easy, but I'm finding out that there are a lot of details I must know that I don't. Like what year the Fair Housing Act was passed. It was 1968 if you're curious. Anyway, John wants me to come over later to go over the plans.

John lives far out in the country in a small old farmhouse, and when I arrive, I meet his roommate, who is also a builder, and his roommate's girlfriend. They're fixing dinner and invite us to eat with them in the tiny little kitchen with low ceilings that would take only two of us, arm's length to arm's length to touch both walls, but instead of feeling cramped It feels cozy and warm.

Starving, I gratefully accept. I had met Gene, his roommate, one time before, while out for lunch with John. Gene's girlfriend Michelle has just moved to town from Denver. She is tall and beautiful and about ten years younger than me. We begin talking when suddenly I realize how refreshing it is to have a conversation that's not about work or children.

I'm really enjoying myself so much that I even forget what I came to do. I feel so comfortable with all of them that I'm actually having fun. I'm a little embarrassed to say that I'm excited that Michelle gave me her number, I think I have a new friend and I'm quite pleased about that.

John's correct, my basement renovation is going along perfectly, and Michelle and I have been hanging out. Last month, I drove her to New Jersey to get some of her things at her parents' house. I've been listening to her for weeks complain about her job and learn on our trip that she has a bachelor's degree in photography from a very prestigious school and is heavily in debt with student loans.

She's moved into a one-bedroom apartment and has nothing. I buy her a sofa and help her make a table. On our ride, I have an idea. *Why doesn't she get her real estate license?* I think we could make really good money together as a real estate team. I'm good at getting listings and she could take the photographs and drive buyers around.

I believe it could really work. She says she wants to but doesn't really have any money to live on while we get started. I'm all cashed up from selling my last house, tell her that I can help her out with money, and since I'm recently graduated I've already started getting listings etc., so by the time she gets her license, I'll be nine months in, we should have houses selling, and we'll split everything.

She says she's in, but I'm not sure if it's because she hates her job. I'm excited because I like hanging out with her, and it'll be nice to have someone helping me with anything. She's talked about how she's made money for all of her past employers, and she's been wanting to do that for herself. I think she'll work just as hard as I do, and I believe this could work, and maybe we could have some fun along the way. She's also mentioned, that she has received the most disgruntled employee award. I laugh. I always find her to be lovely.

THE STORIES THAT WE TELL
Circa 2007

For the past nine months, I've been working as hard as I can getting listings and investing about a grand a month for full page ads to get those houses sold. I'm just breaking even on all my expenses and what I'm bringing in. I'm living off of the cash I have on hand, but with all of my investments and businesses I know that happens at first. You have to put in the time and effort before you get any returns.

Michelle graduated and has joined the same firm as me. She and Gene have broken up, but they've agreed to be partners in a timber frame construction business that he's starting. She's excited about this because she said she's always liked working with numbers. I give her cash to keep her afloat for a while, like previously agreed, but she seems to be focusing more on the business with Gene, than ours.

Sales are coming in from the listings and I'm splitting the commissions with her, but I'm still paying for all the advertisements on of my end. I mention this to her which is hard because she's my friend. She says she's working, but you know how that is when you don't actually see people working you don't know if they are. She hasn't had any sales or listing, but that doesn't mean she's not putting in effort. I know I've worked a lot in many directions with no results.

The store is still doing well. It has grown by leaps and bounds, tripling the sales from each year before, and I know it's because of Jason and the other employees. It pays for itself, but I still only make enough for dinner out, which I use every Monday night with the boys from the store.

We're sponsoring a sports talk radio show with the local radio station, and it's set up to broadcast LIVE from the restaurant. It's been fun too, and I've been happy to have a night out. One night the broadcasters asked Justin and me to come chat with them. Justin was a natural, but when it came to me, I literally froze.

I couldn't speak to answer a question on air. Justin had to jump in for me. A month later, they were having us come to the radio station for a free announcement wishing everyone Happy Holidays from our store as a free perk for us. I went in and nailed it first try, I knew just what I wanted to say.

The promoter for the radio station was really excited like "WOW, that was awesome." He says, "Try introducing this song from Lynyrd Skynyrd." And I froze again. I don't know why. He asked me three times to say it, and I couldn't.

Justin tells me that he thinks he's going to move. He's been working at the store for several years now, and he knows that it's not what he wants to do forever. He and his wife are just going to travel around the country and see where they end up.

Justin's been driving my red BMW Z3 convertible that I bought on the very same day I bought a suit for him to get married in. I love it because it's red and the title said it was originally bought on Valentine's Day. I spent more time that day with Justin buying his suit, than I did buying the car.

So, when I bought it, I was totally thinking of love. When he came back from his honeymoon with his new wife, from New Jersey, they only had the one old blue Subaru to share. I couldn't pay him more money, so I let him use my car and I thought it looked good and brought attention sitting out in front of the store.

It wasn't being used at home and after the closing the warehouse it was the only thing I had left after all the bills were paid. I was looking forward to having the car back at some point, but worried about who would be able to run the store. I really wanted fewer complications in my life, so I came up with another plan. and asked him to help me sell the store, and if he did, I'd help him out financially when he leaves. Excitedly, he agrees.

Sean, one of our employees at the vitamin store, who I love, buys the business with his father. I'm so excited for him. He reminds me a little of me, quiet, reserved, a deep thinker, a little philosophical, gets things done, but also like me, he doesn't speak up and I don't really know what he's thinking.

I think this will be great for him. He knows the business and the products. But when I go to visit the store after it's sold, I immediately sense the change. It feels so much different, but when I look around the store, everything looks the same, but there is an energy pushing me out the door like I should leave. It may be coming from his father, I don't know, I've always been sensitive to energy like this but never really understanding it. I want to visit and chat, but it doesn't feel right.

Michelle has some people she wants to show houses to but she suggests that her car is too old and too small, so I let her use mine, and I can't help but think as I drive her car how it doesn't seem right that I have two really nice cars, and yet I'm driving this old Saturn, with a broken windshield. So after, I finance a car for Michelle, I don't ever want to be without my own car again.

Justin has left on his adventure and John is finishing up my basement. Max, now fifteen, seems different. I don't know what's going on with him. A year or two ago he asked if he could split time between mine and his dad's house wanting to be more around the boys in his father's neighborhood. I get it.

He says there is girl stuff all around my house; the music, the tv shows, the conversation, so reluctantly I say ok, because I don't want him to go, I'll be losing precious time I have with him. I'm really worried though. We're always so on the go, I wish I had more time. Ally wants to do the opposite of Max, but I tell her she has to go with her brother. You need to be together. Which I believe to be true, but it's also because I work longer hours when I don't have them, in order to spend some time with them when I do. It just wouldn't work out.

John, knowing I have money from the sale of the store says "I was looking for some property, and came across a guy who bought some land at auction, and wants to quickly turn it around for a profit. He asked if I knew of anyone who may be interested, and I thought of you." "I'll check it out," I say curiously with a kind of shrug, "When can I see it?"

I now, am not only a Realtor, but an ECO Consultant, a member of the Green Building Council, and the Environmental Consultants Association. A member of the Commercial Investment Realty, the Home Builders Association as well as becoming an elected board member of the Association. True to form, I dive in.

Turning my real estate hobby, for what I hope is a rewarding career, hearing the jingle in my head as I write that down. I find myself again spread thin. Feeling however, like a true entrepreneur, I check out the land that John had told me about. The deed says it's eighty plus or minus acres, and I enjoy reading the description of the land.

It reads, "*Beginning on a stake near a rock culvert in the road, then returning 150 feet to a White Oak, then east 100 feet to a Chestnut tree running along the stream up to...*" it seems so quaint as I drive up an old road to an old family cemetery dating back to the 1850's where the property begins.

The acreage sits in the middle of hundreds of untouched acres, so it makes the land feel even larger. I walk up the path. There is an old logging road from at least fifty years ago. The forest is dense and thick with very large trees, but I make my way through. It's beautiful, and part of the property touches a small town. I think it's a good investment.

A new development is being built close to where I live now. I think it's a good place for my next house, it will take a few months for it to be built so I think the timing will be perfect. I know it's going to be a money maker. I tell my mom and my stepfather about it, and they think it's such a good idea that I help them pre-purchase two homes.

Then they tell a friend who does the same. I don't make any commission on these homes, but I do think they are a great value. John gives me a hard time and says I should build a house with him. He says, "I always wanted to build a timber frame with roommate Gene, we should do that." I put that in the back of my mind for another day.

A realtor calls and tells me that he just got a new listing of forty acres that touches my property, and I quickly realize after looking at the topography, that buying this land will make my acreage so much more valuable. It would give me two ways of entering and leaving the property, and buildable ridge top acres with what I believe will be an amazing view, making it way more valuable.

I believe that I must get it. I put an offer paying four times what I paid for the eighty acres, which is as low as they will go, but feel it's necessary to make my original acreage more valuable. Whether I want to sell it or develop it, it's something I should really do.

There are a few problems with the title to this land however, It's family land that's been in their name for generations, the seller is represented by one of the family members who is also an attorney, they ask for time to get this settled and I agree, we extend the contract.

It turns out that the eighty plus or minus acres, is really a minus. Some of the deed is in question. I'm having both properties surveyed. The former owner of the eighty acres has tracked me down and has been harassing me as if I did this to him, as if I caused him to lose the land.

He keeps calling me on the phone, sending me letters. He's claiming that I stole the property from him. He even showed up at my office. I'm feeling very anxious about this. He lives next to the eighty acres, at a neighboring property near the cemetery, so I have to drive by his house to get to my land, and now I'm a little afraid too. I'm really glad I'm buying this other forty acres so that I have another way in.

Out of the blue, I get an email from Daniel. I'm super excited because I still think about him all the time. It reads, Dr. Wonderful looking for land. I don't know if he's flirting with me or really looking for land. Either way I'm excited. I could use a sale and a date.

You won't believe how many weirdos come out of the woodwork first when you become single and then when you become a realtor. I mean like your friend's married uncle, it's gross. They call you up under the ruse that they have some land they want to sell, or land they want to buy, and then when they get around you they begin fishing, by asking you questions to see if you'll take the bait and then be with them.

I'm hoping they really want to do some business. I always could use a sale, but so far, every time it's turned out to be wasting my already limited time. A couple emailed me that they wanted to look at properties in the area on Mother's Day. I had Max and Ally that day, but I agreed to take them, because of course that's what a realtor is supposed to do.

Plus, I had received the referral from my company, and I had to report back what the status was. Anyway, I spent the whole day with them, morning to dinner time, while my kids sat home alone, showing them all the properties, they wanted to see. Traversing all over three counties.

They were not interested in putting in an offer that day, and I haven't heard from them since. I have a feeling that they just wanted a free tour of the area. But, back to Dr. Wonderful, I message him back and I still can't tell if he's flirting with me or really looking for land. After three replies his messages just stop, leading me nowhere. Ain't nobody got time for this.

A few months later Justin and Ann move back, they've traveled around the country and I'm the last stop. They believe they want to stay in Asheville, and they both want to go back to school. I offer up my fully furnished and newly finished basement, with bedroom, bath, living area, and mini refrigerator and sink, for them to stay in a few months while they save up some money and get settled.

It's kind of nice having them here. My house is beginning to feel a little happier, with Michelle hanging out as well. We have movie nights, and Sunday morning brunches.

My next house that I've invested in the new subdivision is ready, and I was right, it's already worth $50,000 more than I paid, but the house I'm living in hasn't sold yet, so I put renters in on a month to month basis, they are building a house in a really exclusive subdivision and they hope that their house will be ready soon, so it should work out well.

In the meantime, my mother and her friend who have bought houses in the same subdivision, have me find renters for their homes. It's not something I want to do. The real estate company I work for doesn't do rentals, and I'm not going to charge my family or their friends so reluctantly, I do this for them for free.

At the same time a long-lost relative reaches out to me after finding my father. She's doing research about our family. She's from that wealthy branch of the family in NYC and would like a copy of everything I have on our history. My mother has given me all the records.

I believe I even have a pamphlet from her father's college graduation, as my dad's aunt had attended it. So reluctantly I do this as well, taking time to physically photocopy everything I have. A month later she does not send me a thank you or anything but keeps calling me requesting the originals of several items. I don't respond. I'm really getting sick of the sound of the phone ringing. Everyone wants something from me. I don't seem to ever want to answer anymore. Which is bad when you're a realtor. Why can't everybody just take care of their own stuff?

THE STORIES THAT WE TELL
Circa 2006

I've agreed to build a timber frame house with John and Gene, it's already taking longer than expected, and we haven't even begun. I've signed a contract with John and taken out a bank loan. A loan that typically takes two or three weeks for approval, has taken much longer.

The underwriter didn't seem to understand what a timber frame home is. Six months go by after sending the bank an excessive amount of information, before the loan finally goes through, excitedly I drive by the site the next day. It's going to be in a golf course community.

One of the few gated communities in our area. I personally really dislike gated communities but out of state buyers, especially from Florida, love them. But there's a problem with the road leading up to the lot in this twenty-year-old established community, it literally has just washed out. Who knows how long it will take to stabilize the ground and reestablish a road? I call the bank and John, the builder.

The bank surprisingly has said that if I find another lot, I can just change the loan to include a new lot. John suggests a lot that he owns next to a home that he's currently building in same the subdivision. I think that could be a good idea for resale down the road to have two timber frame homes close to each other, but it's on the backside of the mountain and far away from the front gate and all activities.

There is a back gate, but it's unmanned and out of the way, and doesn't always work. Leaving you to drive twenty minutes around the mountain to the main entrance. The seclusion however, of this very wooded area could work for someone looking for this style home.

John meets me at the property, and we walk down a very steep mountainside from the road. I laugh as we get to the bottom of the property.

"John, this is never going to work."

He says, "Look how beautiful it is down here. It's level, and it's like being in the forest."

He's really super excited about it and thinks it will be great! And, his excitement gets me excited. I can see what he's saying, a house in this spot would be beautiful. I notify the bank, but now we're all sitting here at my dining room table, months later and nothing has been done and no one seems to be talking.

Apparently, the loan gives a $50,000 advance for a partial purchase for timbers to be used, John doesn't want to give it to Gene until after the material is here, and Gene can't order it without it. Gene doesn't think it's ever really going to happen. I tell him, I already have a loan, I already have paid for plans. Everything is approved. Time is ticking. Knowing that I'm already way behind. This is how I'm earn money. No one is talking, I don't know what's happening behind the scenes, but I need to get this moving, so I grab my checkbook and write Gene a check. "Can we get this going now," I ask.

My house finally sells, and Michelle and I split the commission from it, continually trying to prove to her that I believe in what we're doing, and I believe we can make money if we work at it. I've been able to get us a growing list of listings. I want to keep her motivated, but I don't feel like she's with me.

Justin and Ann have moved into their own place and are doing well. I want to move into the smaller four-bedroom, 2.5 bath home that I've purchased and put the renters in, but unfortunately their house has not been going as planned as well and has been taking a lot longer than expected.

They think they only need another month or two. Me not wanting to put them out, even though they are on a month to month contract, tell them that they can stay, because you know I'm tough, and I'm use to moving nine hundred times, so, no-no I don't want to put anyone else out, and moving the contents of a whole house is SOOO inexpensive and fun.

And, YES, I'm speaking sarcastically. I rent my mother's friend's house that is in the same neighborhood, and available. They've agreed to let me stay for just a few months. And, true to their word my renters' house finishes, two months later I move in.

Upon moving in however, I step into a hole while carrying a pot around to the back of the house. I hear a loud pop, I'm down on the ground and in so much pain. I have to crawl into the house. I never went to the doctors and two weeks ago I let my insurance go after paying for twenty some years without use.

For the next two weeks, I'm stuck on the lower floor, with no bedroom, no refrigerator, and only a half bath, so every night, I'm crawling up the stairs to go to sleep. It's a week, I don't have my children, but my fabulous son stops by without me asking, and brings me some much-needed food, I order a refrigerator online. But, is the universe trying to tell me something? I have so much to do but, I'm stuck on the couch. I don't think I can handle feeling any sorrier for myself.

Just before my accident, an uncle of a friend called and said that their friend had a house to rent and asked if I knew of anyone who needed a house to let them know, because the owner was going out of the country. I believe he may have been trying to set us up as he was a single guy.

Anyway, almost immediately after putting the phone down, an old friend called and said they had a friend, whose child was coming into town for a few months, and asked if I knew of a place, so of course I told them that, "Yeah I know of a place." And since again my company does not do rentals, I was just helping my friends of friends connect, but it has somehow left me coordinating all of it, since the owner of the home is heading out of town.

Now I'm having to call in a favor and call my builder friend John to go help them with the hot water heater that isn't working for the same reason, and also ask if I will let them in. I guess I didn't make it clear that I'm doing this all for free and I'm injured, but I somehow make it there and thank John, who's helping his friend, who's helping friends of friends.

John's girlfriend is not happy with my occasional calls for help. I'm just used to calling him after finishing my basement and now while we are building a home. We've had a lot of discussions. I really feel like he's a brother. I'm mad at him most of the time. He's really putting me in a bad situation with this timber frame.

Later, it turns out that the owner of the rental property had a live-in girlfriend before he rented it out and left town. Now she's back, calling my boss and accusing me of having an affair with him. I really just can't catch a break. Which stings, when you truly want someone in your life, and you've been alone for so long. I'm remembering the saying that, "No good deed goes unpunished kind of thing." I really need to stop being so nice.

The housing market is slowing down, but I'm not too concerned.

DONNA MELANSON

What I've noticed from watching and investing in real estate for the last twenty years is that we're a little insulated here in the mountains of Western North Carolina. We don't seem to be affected like the rest of the country when it comes to downturns.

John and I seem to have a different way of doing things. He's trying to find the cheapest way to build the home, while still using the best of everything in materials and craftsmanship. I agree, but I also know time is money so sometimes paying a little more for both the material and craftsmen to complete the job quicker, I believe is better, especially since the interest payments are mounting on this construction loan. John and I are supposed to be partnering on this home but somehow, I'm holding all the risk as he's worked into the loan payments to himself. I know he needs to feed his family but so do I.

I've become more involved with the Home Builder's Association, it's taking up so much time but, I think it's a good investment. I've decided to tell Michelle that it's not working out with our partnership. We're just now getting ready to close on the first property that she's sold, and she hasn't added any listings.

I'm not sure what she's been doing, but I know that I've also tried many things without the results that I've wanted. Like, I wish I was selling more too. It's just that she said she could do so much, and I was actually looking for help which is why I wanted to partner with her, and instead I still feel like I'm employing her.

It really hurt too when we had another delay on the timber frame house, and she said that they, meaning her and Gene, didn't want to do something for the timber frame house because of John. I said, "But this is my house." I thought to myself, *haven't I done enough for you Michelle. I built this house with you. In hopes that all of us could prosper. I supported you in real estate, I helped you out in so many personal ways, and you can't see how this is hurting me here, by delaying me more?*

I don't want to feel that responsibility of helping anymore. But I don't say any of that out loud. I don't know why I'm so bad at communicating. I really tried to help her. I just can't handle this feeling anymore of continually supporting others and not being supported. It wasn't my finest moment. Me, not always able to speak my truth, thinking she should know why, when she doesn't seem to. She wants to talk about it. I'm not able to say what I'm thinking in a kind way, and I have nine hundred thoughts running through my head on everything that I'm continually juggling that words don't come out. So, I don't say anything other than a really surprisingly loud "I love you," and I say it at our office as I'm walking out the door.

On more than one occasion it's been brought to our awareness, that our co-workers think we're lesbians. One night we were invited to a Jazz club. We should have known something was up when we saw a bowl full of condoms on the way in. Let's just say the experience was humorous and traumatic at the same time.

SO much drama in this particular gay bar, on this particular night, couples and ex's, and sugar daddies, and really, really bad Jazz, not the cool kind, but the "You light up my life" kind. We ended up having to go to another bar after and ordered bourbon - straight up.

We laughed after always seeming to find ourselves in these situations, but we really did have fun together, and having fun was something that hadn't happened for me in a really long time. It was also sad because both of us were really looking for love.

Another time, we went to Florida to visit my family after the holidays. My dad brought up the conversation of being gay and said he thought it was a fad. I argued back that people are who they are at birth. I know this to be true especially after raising two children.

Both of them with same IQ, both of them raised in the same households, but I kept trying to get one of them to loosen up a little bit, and the other to get more serious, neither one of them ever budged one inch from who they are.

I ask my father if he could ever be with a man. He said no, never. So, I asked, "How do you think, then, that it could be a fad?" He asked if I was, and I said no, I don't believe I ever could be with a woman. I'm really attracted to men. I thought it was the end of the discussion. Until my stepmom came home. He practically shouted into the other room, "BEVERLY, I talked to Donna, she said she could never be with a woman," and he seemed quite proud of that.

When my conversation with Michelle ends, I'm embarrassed with this thought of my I love you, that was a little louder than it should have been, and of more people thinking I'm a lesbian, not there is anything wrong with that, it's just when you identify one way, you just don't want people to identify you another way. You just want to be you.

John is here picking me up. It doesn't feel right that my conversation with Michelle is cut short, and that I don't have time to explain myself or my thoughts or even wait for her to reply. While I'm leaving the office to go on this errand with John, who is not on my or Michelle's good list. Like the majority of my life over the last twenty years, everything just feels wrong.

THE STORIES THAT WE TELL
Circa 2007

My ex uncle-in-law calls me up with a really big commercial listing on airport road. It's mine if I go to the office of a friend of his who is starting a new real estate company, so I do. It's too good an opportunity to pass up. And, at the real estate company I meet a lot of new people.

Among them is a forester who dabbles in real estate on the side, and surprisingly a loan officer on site that just happens to be the father of one of my daughter's soccer teammates. Both owners of the company sell real estate, so the company hires a manager to run it.

I like him, but he just moved to the area and at every single sales meeting he keeps talking about doom and gloom in the real estate market. I keep thinking he doesn't know what he's talking about. I know we've all been feeling a little downturn in the housing market, but we've always been a little insulated in Asheville from what goes on around the country.

Areas around the country are starting to report that they're experience a slump in the housing, but everything around here seems to be going well enough. It's hard to keep hearing, however, as I'm still struggling with all my daily stresses.

Michelle is still working in the timber frame business and has started a small bookkeeper business for people like the timber framer who has skills and passion to grow a business but not the time or desire for the accounting of it. It's much needed and I think it's what she's really wanted to do.

My timber frame is almost finished. I put it on the market for way more than I thought I would ever have to, but John has spent too much money on the build, probably because of the steep lot that it's on. So, I find myself coming out of pocket for kitchen and bathroom cabinets, counter tops, landscaping and a very long driveway. It's a $60,000 blow, really diminishing my bank account as are the monthly mortgage payments. Switching real estate companies has also really hurt my income.

Henry and Sharon are two new clients from Florida who're actively trying to buy a house whenever they're in town. I'm so grateful because they're looking for a house over a million, and since I work on commission it would really help right now. We keep looking at many houses, and in this price range the days the houses that have been on the market are high.

My client keeps low balling everyone with the awareness that he's just afraid of what may come with the economy and is trying to protect his interest. Looking at the statistics I support this, but understand when no one is taking the bait, because, like me, after living in this area for many years you understand that we have for whatever reason been a little protected from these trends.

After two years, the owner of the forty acres that is adjacent to my eighty acres says he's almost ready to close, so I pay to have the property surveyed again. I'm not sure how I'm going to be able to pay for this property now, I don't think conventional financing is going to work since I'm already holding two mortgages and have had very little income.

This timber frame house is kicking my butt and has just been a continual drain on my bank account. I talk to Sal, the soccer dad in my office. He's just moved from South Florida and knows a few private lenders. He hooks me up with a few people and I speak to them of what I'm trying to do with the land. Only one of them is interested and he happens to be coming to my area in about a month. He has a friend who lives here. We plan a meeting and a trip to the property.

I've been talking to Jim, the forester in my office about my land. He wants to see it. So, I take him out there, and tell him what I want to do. He suggests selectively harvesting the timber. He says it would be good for the environment as it's just too dense, and it would enable me to cut a road in from the other side therefore by passing the crazy ex landowner.

I think it's a great idea, because I truly believe at the top of the ridge of this mountain where the two properties meet, that they'll be some amazing views, making the land even more valuable. I meet the prospective investor in the property at the parking lot of a grocery store located near his friend.

He gets into my car, and I begin to tell him all about the eighty plus or minus acres that I own and the forty acres I want to purchase as we drive towards the property and up the old logging road on the original eighty acres. It's dark as we drive well into the forest. Up ahead we come to a fallen tree.

We get out of the car and walk the rest of the way up to the highest point. I explain that this is where the two properties meet at the top of this ridge, and went on to tell him that the forty acres are too dense to walk but describe how I would like to develop the south side of the ridge with small environmentally sustainable houses that are clustered together in groups, and on the top of the ridge, and the northside sell lots in acreage size for larger homes.

Then I fill him in on a lot of other things about the property, like the location of water and sewer and the environmental study that I had completed. I inform him that part of my land is in this small cities district where I learned, a long time ago, does provide water and sewer to its residences and even has a mandatory requirement for connecting to its systems, which is great for what I'm trying to create.

What I've learned recently, however, is that they seem to be having a water shortage and can't service any more homes. The solution I believe could be to create our own water system on my property, that can hook into the system that's in place, effectively helping to lessen the load of the city.

Then, I tell him that I'm not sure I want to go forward with it now. I'm feeling uneasy and unsure which is not like me. Sure, overworked, over tired, sad, unloved, yes, but unsure of business - no. I'm fully in touch with this area of my life. I don't tell him that, but I do tell him that I own the eighty acres out right, and not sure I want to put it up as collateral.

He said he admired and respected the fact that I didn't and went on to tell me that I reminded him of a developer that he backed on some small hotels in South Beach - Miami, and then later on a hotel in Las Vegas. Flattered, my ego must have overtaken my tired reasoning mind, because later I decide to go forward with the purchase of the land.

I've also joined the parade of homes committee with the Home Builders Association. Secretly thinking it would be great if one day we could use the property as a parade of homes community, instead of everyone traveling all over three counties to see the different homes.

I think at some point I'll propose lots that can be purchased by builders, but to be paid for at time of sale of finished houses. As an elected board member of the association. I wonder if it would be seen as a conflict of interest. Nevertheless, it could work for everyone's benefit. Anyway, this committee is taking up far more time than I had anticipated.

I employ to have an aerial topography completed of my land, and a landscape architect to plat out lots. The forester creates an entrance to the property and begins a sustainable harvesting of timber. I allow two young men everyone in town calls the "dirty boys," to move into a falling down farm workers house that sits at the road.

The house is far from livable, but it does have a good roof and they are happy to be able to stay there. They claim they will help fix it up for me. We'll see what they can do. They definitely can't make it any worse. There is no electricity or running water in the house, but a small creek is near.

The house is set on piers made from stones that look like they are ready to fall down, and there's a hole in the floor where the bathroom's supposed to be. I buy a fifty-gallon drum that's fitted with a water spigot at the bottom, and a screen at the top. I drop it off at the house for the dirty boys so that they can use the gutter to collect rainwater.

The community is really small here, and I seem to be getting to know everyone. Turns out the magistrate is also a builder. While visiting him in his office I find out that besides his home he has in town, he also has a small camp far outside of town, at a property he owns. I'm fascinated as he talks about creating electricity using a miniature water wheel in a stream nearby, and at the same time with just a pause in our conversation I become a witness to a couple getting married whose names I do not know.

I was also able to visit a couple who lived off the grid. The husband literally wrote the book on green building. They live in a passive solar home, where sunlight comes in and heats the stone of the floors and then the stones radiate heat throughout the day and

100   DONNA MELANSON

night. The walls of the home are made out of straw and mud, and the toilet is simply filled with wood shavings.

A local shop owner took me out to a couple's property that was way out in the country. I believe he said they have three hundred acres and have been living off the grid since the nineteen seventies. I hate to stereotype, but I see a photograph hanging on the wall from that time period of them on a snow-covered day, standing in front of their home with a VW van beside them.

The bathtub is in the kitchen and they still heat the water from the stove. The husband, I learn is a Harvard grad, he's built their home strictly from materials from the land only, and I cannot put into words the artistry of his carpentry skills. It's so beautifully made. Admiringly I touched the wood, it feels as soft and smooth as butter, like the whole house is a finely crafted piece of furniture. My heart feels as if it can explode as if it's growing with love for this place and I never want to leave.

I don't know why, but I have a real affinity for wood and natural products. It's almost like they are alive, and I can feel energy coming from them speaking to me. I love finely crafted furniture, and hand carved wood frames that cover mirrors and art. It's such a stark contrast to what I grew up with in South Florida, with palm trees and pavement.

A year goes by and everything is different and yet the same. I've spent so much money and time on the land, getting it ready. Phase one complete. Sharon and Henry, the couple making the million-dollar home purchase are still looking, and my timber frame still hasn't sold. The smaller house that I'm living in off of Longfellow road hasn't sold either. I think Henry might have been right all along. I think the housing crisis is coming and I believe it's going to hit here. I'm feeling it.

My friend and fellow soccer mom Liz has asked me to list her home. It's priced a little over a million dollars and it's in one of the preferred neighborhoods that Henry and Sharon really want, so I bring them to it. They really like it, but Henry makes one of his low offers. Liz has told me that they really need to sell, but they don't want to go that low. My money is getting really tight too and I really could use the double sale, but Liz has been my friend for years and Sharon, Henry and I have become very close since we've been looking for a home for them for over a year.

As I work with both couples, I begin to feel like I really just want to help them all out, so I do what no realtor should. I give them each other's information, to see if they can work out a deal without having to pay commission. Luckily for me, they still can't make a deal. I don't believe Liz and her husband have a sense of what is coming with the economy. I'm trying to help.

At the office the mood has gotten low. I feel it personally and professionally. I keep working but I haven't had any income in a long time. Money is pouring out of my accounts, and I'm juggling many different things. Today, on top of the downward spiraling economy, my boss tells me that he feels bad for me because I seem sad, and he says he knows I'm going home alone every night.

I'm acutely aware of all of this, but now I also feel the pain that he feels for me, and it makes it worse, if it's even possible, but I appreciate that he truly means it in a sincere concern for me.

The house next door to Liz goes up on the market. It's a bigger home and on a bigger lot. It's also priced a little more. I immediately show it to Sharon and Henry. The owners of the home have already moved out. I don't know if they themselves have been affected by this looming downturn but when Henry comes in with his low offer, the sellers take it, and now they'll be Liz's neighbor, and she's not too excited about it.

Her home's value has just dropped by this sale. I'm, however, so grateful for the sale and so is my boss. When you list with a real estate company, the commission is typically split between the listing and selling agents and then the agents have to split the commission with the company they have signed on with. So, this sale has helped many. It couldn't have come at a better time.

I feel like I need to make a change. I don't want to work for this company anymore. None of my great commercial or residential listings have sold, and I can't handle the mood here. Everyone is down and it's just too painful. I have enough trouble keeping myself pumped up.

I'm switching to an environmental real estate company where the mood is positive. Most of the listings are with green building, and because I love nature, I'm hoping the vibe will be a good place for me to be. Most of my listings are about due for a renewal, so I'm able to bring a few with me. I worked hard trying to sell them, having open houses, giving night and weekend showings, investing in advertising, but nothing came of it. My friend Liz lists with another company when I switch. I sincerely feel I did my best.

John calls me out of the blue. We really haven't been talking to each other since the house was finished a year ago. I know his girlfriend, now fiancé, isn't very comfortable with me being his friend, but I haven't talked to him in months. I've just been sitting on the house, paying the mortgage. He asks, however, if I'll do him a favor. I don't want to since I'm still really mad at the situation I'm in with the timber frame house, but apparently, I can never say no, and say sure, what the heck, what do you need?

He says, "I need you to call my fiancé and tell her we are not having an affair."

"An affair, why does she think we're having an affair?" I ask.

"She's found some old photos of us from that trip we took a long time ago, along with some condoms I had in an old backpack."

Reluctantly, I call.

It's funny in a very painstaking way that I'm being grilled by a woman about something that's so far from the truth, and she's not believing me. I tell her that it's been months and months since there has been anybody in my life. I just sit at home reading self- help books alone, and John is more like my brother.

I'm mad at him most of the time, but she's not listening to anything I say. And, it's getting harder to hear her berate me, as I sit alone in my house for the umpteenth night. Where all I do is try to take care of my family, and help everyone, in any way that I can.

I have more things to deal with than a silly, insecure woman. The timber frame isn't selling, in fact, nothing seems to be selling. My funds are depleting to a very low level since I'm paying for everything with a pretty much non-existent income. I'm not sure what to do, but I've always been able to see my way forward.

It's helped me to organize, grow my businesses and maintain my household, but I'm not seeing a way out. I mean I do, if the land, which I listed a few months ago, or houses sell, but I don't foresee any of that happening. For over a year and a half I've been skeptical of Henry's forecast, because of my ability to see forward, but now I believe he is right, nothing is selling.

To give myself more time and lessen the drain on my bank account, I begin looking for a renter, and quickly find a couple to rent my home, but they need it in three days. Ally, my beautiful daughter who's now in high school, helps me pack. We'll be moving on the fourth of July.

I hope, ... I know, I can make this happen. We're experienced movers, and I know Max will help with the move too. The income from the rental home will pay that mortgage and I believe staging the timber frame with us in it, may help it show better.

Fingers crossed; I need something to sell!

PART TWO

LOVE YOURSELF

Where this Story Began

LOVE YOURSELF

A long year later, and where this story originally began, I just begin...changing.

Am I going insane or just becoming sane? That question lingers in my mind, as I sit here debating my future path. I know what I want to do, and I know what my heart is calling me to do, and in that sense, I feel completely sane and completely alive. I'm, however, still enjoying all the luxuries that my old path has provided. A path that I feel if I continue, will suck that last bit of life out of me.

The insanity in question is turning my back on what I've always done, and what knowingly provides me food, shelter, and all the other necessities of life. But it all seems strangely unimportant right now, but that's so easy to say when you're not physically, at the moment, suffering from hunger and cold, and yet, I feel like it's something that I have to do. Like my life can't take another path until this mission is done.

My reality continues to be that I feel like a pawn, that has been played in this nightmare called my life. That I have jumped into many different games, playing many different positions in life, thinking these are the things I should be doing. Trying to play, trying to lead, giving it my all, only time and time again being weakened by the effort.

It's almost as if everyone was playing around me - like they could see me, but I wasn't supposed to be there. But I kept trying. I kept unpacking my gear, talking to the other players, making myself known and wondering why I was there, with no one reacting to my efforts, they just kept doing what they were doing, knowing that I didn't belong.

They would smile and be polite. I would race around, running in circles, doing good deeds - giving, giving, giving, and trying to find my place. Now at this crossroad where I'm facing my total financial demise, I will lose everything I've worked for. The logical side of me says get any job you can, you need to feed yourself and your children, but I can't do it in this town that has not embraced me, where my generosity has left me empty, I just want to lay down and die. More torture that I just don't think I can handle. I'm a survivor though, without thinking, I stand back up.

I forgot to have dreams, is that where I went wrong? I spent all my time fitting myself in society and other people's dreams of what I should do, that I forgot to think about what it is that I want. What will make me happy? What does my perfect life look like? In the back of my mind, I believe I've been thinking about this for a couple of years now. I know I've not been happy. Depressed is probably the right word. Grieving for the loss of my life and decisions that I've made.

I've begun asking myself daily - what would my perfect life even look like? And, it's been surprisingly hard trying to figure it out, but, since I'm using my imagination, I've now given myself permission to think that I can have anything I want. Because for some reason I have this need to rationalize how this "anything" can be possible.

I've asked myself: what if you won the lottery and you didn't have to worry about money? How would you spend your time? What is your soul calling you to do? And, this perspective has made it so much easier, because I'm not thinking about excuses, or money, or logistics, nothing other than, what do I want?

My answer surprises me, seeing that I'm emotionally at the lowest point in my life. Or maybe it's precisely because I'm at the lowest part of my life, that even if I had all the money in the world, my soul's desire is that I want to inspire others, I want to travel, and I want to write. And, now I have this insatiable urge to tell my story. Which, I also think is crazy.

My life is falling apart in every possible way, I'm single and alone, a real estate job with no income, and I'm about to lose every material possession that I own. I failed English twice in college and I've felt sad for the last twenty years, so I don't think I'm wrong in being surprised by my answer of wanting to write, travel and inspire others. And, at the same time my answer feels honest and true for me. I do believe, however, that it's possible - why not, I think anything is possible, maybe that's my superpower.

I want to start living this life now, obviously, I mean, who wants to live sad and in fear? I desperately need my life to change, all of it. I can't keep living the way I've been living. So, I'm going to love myself and just begin.

I start by writing a positive inspiring blog. Simply for the pure pleasure of living my life in a new way, and if nothing else, at least it will help me focus on something positive for a change. I need positive words, thoughts, ideas, ... I need everything right now to be positive! I really can't handle anything else.

In addition to writing Goldilocks Blog, and through the ever-powerful chant that I've been hearing in my head of *YO-GA, YO-GA, YO-GA,* I've begun practicing yoga and meditation at home, and I have to say that it's making a huge difference in my life. For the first time, other than being on the mountain, I feel a moment of peace.

I keep hoping that I can carry this feeling with me all day, but it hasn't happened yet. Sometimes it doesn't last for more than five minutes. But I'll take whatever little moments of peace that I can get.

I have to live differently, because my old way of living isn't working for me anymore. Although I'm not sure it ever was.

In addition to the blog, the yoga, the meditation, I've also been journaling, a practice that I've done for many years. But now I've been writing an additional paragraph daily: a paragraph that starts off with *"I'm so happy and grateful now that I...."* and, I write this statement in the present tense as if all my desires have already happened.

It's something I learned from Bob Proctor, in my self-help studies, but never put into practice. Now I do, and I find it even more powerful writing after I practice yoga, with the movements, and the breathing, it allows my mind to quiet which is where I'm not only finding peace, but clarity. The positive statement that I write after allows me to dream of the life I want to live, and what I believe will make me happy.

My almost daily practice looks like this.

- *Yoga and Meditation* – *A 30-minute gentle yoga flow video, that's set on a white sand beach. Sitting up after and flowing right into a meditation – just be.*
- *Journal entry* - *Is whatever thoughts are flowing out of my head.*
- *My positive statement set in the present tense. I write about the life I want to have. What does it look like? How do I feel living this life? Etc.*
- *My Blog Post* – *Looking for the good that I have around me now, and writing about whatever I need to inspire myself. I write and post, hoping that it will help others as well.*

This is what one of my positive statements looks like.

Positive Statement in the present tense

I'm so happy and grateful now that I've found the perfect man for me. He's handsome, kind, caring, compassionate. He allows me to be me. He's respectful and he knows me and what I've been through without having to tell him in a deep way. I can breathe with him. I can relax and let go. He's got my back. I write and we travel.

We have lots of friends and family around, and everyone feels at home wherever we are. Our children and he and I are all happy and healthy. We travel all over the world. I live a peaceful, happy, calm life and I inspire others to do the same.

I saw Lorelei the other day and I broke down crying. I thought I was feeling better, but I guess the life I'm trying to live versus my old world came flashing forward the moment I saw her. I didn't understand it at first, how I could be feeling so good, and then triggered so quickly in the next moment to fall so far. It upset me so much that I even told Ally what I was trying to do to change my life with my yoga, meditation and positive statements. Her response was, "You don't believe it then." She's right, but at this stage of my evolution, and at that moment when you're with someone who knows what you've been through, it's hard to believe the new story of the new life I'm creating without anything tangent.

I'm probably going to have to move a few more times after my house goes into foreclosure, and I'm probably going to end up with not owning anything, but I guess you really never do. You just get to have it for a moment and I'm grateful for the moments that I've had. It's just stressful now with all the uncertainty, and creditors calling all the time vs how I've always seen myself as honorable, with an exceptionally perfect credit record.

I hope I've learned my lesson now, that nothing is forever and to enjoy the moment that I'm in. I definitely feel that I did the best that I could. I'm not perfect, I guess none of us are, so I'm going to keep doing the best that I can, with what I have, where I am. I'm going to sincerely try to enjoy every minute of life that I can. I'm going to find the beauty around me, and I'm going to continue loving.

My thought for the day - nurture yourself and surround yourself with nurturing people.

My success so far, is that I am still standing. I'm mentally battered and bruised, but I'm still alive. I've made many choices, which I wish I had not made, but have learned so much along the way that I guess it's all good.

I'm so clever, I think sarcastically, that I've strategically placed myself in the real estate industry, and now I'm in the biggest real estate bubble burst in the history of the United States. I have such great vision! I can make things happen, and I'm smack dab in the thick of things. Yay, I continue to speak sarcastically to myself, knowing that this is just the latest of a lot of not so fabulous events that has happened in my life. Yes, still standing is a success!

To keep going I also pump myself up with quotes like the one from Theodore Roosevelt; *"It is not the critic who counts; not the man who points out how the strong man stumbles, or where the doer of deeds could have done them better. The credit belongs to the man who is actually in the arena, whose face is marred by dust and sweat and blood; who strives valiantly; who errs, who comes short again and again, because there is no effort without error and shortcoming; but who does* actually strive to do the deeds; who knows great enthusiasms, the great devotions; who spends himself in a worthy cause; who at the best knows in the end the triumph of high achievement, and who at the worst, if he fails, at least fails while daring greatly, so that his place shall never be with those cold and timid souls who neither know victory nor defeat."

I wonder if using this quote is just a way to stroke my bruised ego. I use it however, because I need it, so I guess it is. I really want to at least think of myself that way. I need something to hold myself up.

I've put myself out there with all of my heart and soul trying to be a better person, and I feel that my whole self has been marred in the trying, and I've not yet experienced the true triumph of achievement. On the good days, I tell myself, to sit in the pride of at least daring, and, on the bad days... I just feel plain foolish.

I've been diving deeper into self-study, I've always read self-help books at night before going to sleep, but this time it's different, I have to take the time to listen. And I have to say I feel a little fear of trying something yet again, that I may also feel foolish about. You know imposter syndrome, even though for the first time I feel that this is who I am. I'm asking myself; how did I get here? Where do I want to go? What does my perfect life look like? What is the perfect way to live? If I could have everything and anything that I wanted what would that be? This, I believe, is why I became Goldi, the anonymous blogger in search of a perfect life in a perfect world. That way, I can begin living the life I want to live without anyone knowing about it.

I wonder why I'm afraid of feeling foolish again: is anyone even watching? Maybe it's just that I don't want to disappoint myself again. I'll have to sit with that one for a while.

<hr>

As I practice my yoga and meditation and write my Goldilocks Blog on all the self-help and positive things I want to remember, while journaling my current truths, as well as foreshadowing the life I want to live, my life goes back and forth in what is typically thought of as positive and negative. Then slowly, it begins to change. I move into the being and living the life that I want to live. Slowly changing my energy, my mindset, my way of being.

Yoga and Meditation Practice

Journal Entry

Wow! I'm at the real estate office and I was feeling great! But then the phone rang, and it's my mom's friend, who truly needs and deserves help, but I have been helping her for free for four years now. I guess that since I'm having a hard time with taking care of myself right now and knowing that she's going to ask me to do something for her, all she had to do was ask me how I was doing, and I started crying. Yes, right here smack dab in the middle of the office, and the worst part is - I can't stop, ... I guess I have a way to go.

Blog Post

This morning I woke up to the sound of rain. A perfect gentle summer rain, and it sounded sweeter than normal, because the flowers and vegetables in my garden were in desperate need of a drink. By the time I

DONNA MELANSON

got out of bed, the sun was trying to shine through, and by the time the coffee was made, and my cup was poured the sun was shining brightly.

As I gazed out the window, my drink in hand, the trees and flowers seemed so fresh and new and for the first time it really did seem like it was truly the beginning of a brand-new day! It was as if God made it just for me... it was exactly what I needed, rain and the sun to grow and inspire my garden and myself.

Hope you have a beautiful day!
Love Goldi
Goldilocks Blog

Yoga and Meditation Practice

Journal Entry

I woke up this morning with an inspiring dream. I dreamt about love and the pursuit of success. But as I think of it more, the dream really didn't give me either, but did make me feel as if I was getting a little bit closer. And, like all dreams I don't remember everything, but I was looking at a woman and a man, and she had to make a choice between something she wanted to do and the love of this man. She chose the man.

I was also a real estate agent in my dream, and I must have told someone about wanting to write my book, in which I turn my life around and then it has a happy ending. Everyone at the office voted for me for some reason unknown to me, but it made me happy. Then they let everyone go but three people and I was one of the three. So,

I felt excited for the support, and the pressure to make something happen. I could sense that everyone needed this hope.

Then there was a man that I liked. If he chose to eat lunch with me, then that meant he chose me, but if he chose to help me fill a jar with coffee then that meant he chose the project.

I was nervous and the anticipation was killing me. Was a man finally going to choose me, or was I going to have to act okay with the fact that he didn't, but yet still continue to work on the project with him? I looked down at my purse and I was embarrassed because I could see a strip of photographs, the type you get from a machine at the fair or the mall, and I didn't want him to see it because it was photos of him and me, and I wasn't sure he would choose me or my project.

Well, he finally spoke and said, *"We don't have to eat lunch at this moment. We can eat later, can't we?"* So it felt like he was saying, he wasn't sure he wanted me, and I was so upset that it woke me up.

So, no happy ending yet, but maybe success or support for a book, maybe success for love. It's only a dream, but I guess that's closer than I've been.

Blog Post

While visiting family recently, I stopped at a friend's house that was open, bright and clean. This friend really lives her life. She's always on the go and works a really hard and laborious job that is somewhat flexible with time so that she can travel and relax and explore.

Her future is not secure, but she always seems so upbeat, so I ask her; How does she stay so positive? She says with conviction, "I refuse to

DONNA MELANSON

live in fear! Right now, I have everything I need. So, I'm going to enjoy what I have, while I have it, and if something happens, I will deal with it then." I felt so good staying there that I didn't want to leave, but right before it was time for me to go, her sister in law stopped by. I told her how nice it was to see her and asked how she was doing. Her reply was a series of complaints... wow - I couldn't wait to run out the door.

My next stop was at another friend's house. This friend, however, has been sick for as long as I've known her. Nothing serious mind you but sinus infections, aches and pains, that kind of thing. The house was cluttered, and the blinds were drawn, and my friend was constantly saying negative things, but weirdly seemed happy in her own little world. That was who she was, and it was fine with her. She didn't want to change.

It hit me hard. Maybe I was never present enough to actually feel it and really see it, or maybe I just never experienced the two extremes so clearly defined like that, but it really struck a chord with how I want to be in the world. It reminds me that happiness is already within us. We just sometimes need to shift our perception and remember how lucky we are as we focus on actually living life, while being happy with what we have already.

Today is a beautiful day! I have a roof over my head, food in the pantry, and I am alive! I hope I always see the beauty and I hope you do too!

Just a thought...
Love, Goldi

Yoga and Meditation Practice

Journal Entry

- Happiness = Inner Peace
- If It Doesn't Work, Just Do Something Different.
- Relax, Trust, Surrender

I feel like I'm in love. Funny thing is that I'm not dating anyone. The last guy I was kind of seeing was Sam. I met Sam while taking myself out to eat a couple years ago. We did my typical dating pattern of seeing each other once a month. He lives out of state and travels for work. He still randomly calls from time to time but, I'm happy to report that I don't care.

With Sam I've always felt like one of his fishing poles that he really liked but didn't always use. He would put me away somewhere deep into the closet, and when he would think about me again, he would find me behind all of his other stuff. Then he would get excited at the prospect of being with me, enjoy using me tremendously, and then, at the end of the day, he would be sad sometimes when he had to put me away, but he does.

Until he thinks about me again, and when he has free time, and what seems like a moment with nothing else to do. It's confusing as a woman, because you feel the real joy that comes from men when they are with you, the emptiness when you're stuck in the darkness, and the hope of something more.

Nevertheless, Sam, no Sam, or nobody. I feel Love! Is it because Max is doing well, and my daughter may be coming to live with me full time, and we're really connecting? Is it because I'm finally working towards the life I want to live? Is it the yoga and medita-tion that I've been practicing every day? Or, all of the above? I'm not sure. All I know is I'm feeling happy. Not the severe highs and lows that I was feeling before but a pretty steady stream of calm, peaceful happiness.

I think it may be acceptance of what may come, and the fact that I'll be alright. Nothing is forever. I've heard that so many times be-fore, but this time it feels different. Intellectually I've always known nothing is forever, but why does it seem when something ends that we are shocked that it happened?

I was unhappy in my marriage and then surprised and really hurt when it ended. I guess I should look at my life and financial situation the same way. I wasn't happy, even though I was giving it my all. We should try to remember, that it really isn't forever.

We need to remember to take it all in stride with what's to come, good and bad; just keep showing up and doing the best that we can, but maybe we can be better at where we place our efforts. We'll sit back, take a moment and regroup, and then keep moving on, either by choice, or chance, things will definitely change.

I started seeing a therapist a few months ago while I still had a little money. That's the thing when you're single and alone; you really don't have anyone to talk to, period. Whether it's to bounce ideas off of, or to discuss how to handle a situation in parenting, or with customers, or at a time like this, where you feel you may be mentally losing it.

My therapist described this for me by drawing a line across a piece of paper. He said something like this line represents contentment and happiness and most people go in waves a little above the line and a little below the line as things happen in our lives.

Some people have huge waves when they are grieving and coping with loss, and there are some people who stay just below the line, always seeming a little sad. He thought that may be me, and when he described it, I knew that for the last twenty years that it was true. For all of my adult life I've been hovering below the line.

Unhappy with my life and unwilling to even see that it was up to me to change, because I believed that I was working extremely hard, doing everything I thought I was supposed to do, without even a thought that this is *my life* and that I'm in control. If not me, then who?

It reminds me of what I learned in a college psychology class, about the Pavlov experiment with dogs, to see if we can adapt our behavior to a changing environment. This experiment was later expanded on by Martin Seligman. The Pavlov study conditioned dogs to salivate by the sound of a bell in hopes of being fed.

Seligman wanted to see if the conditioning would work with negative conditioning. And I'm sorry for sharing this because he did something really cruel, but it teaches us a great lesson. He shocked the dogs, and he restrained them so they couldn't go anywhere.

After the dogs were conditioned in this way, he built a box with a half wall in the middle so that they could jump from side to side if they desired. But when the dogs were shocked, the dogs remained still resigned to what they felt life had brought them. Proving that you accept what situation that you don't feel like you have control of.

The dogs never tried to jump over. To prove it, they tested the box after to see what a dog would do that had not been conditioned, and the dog jumped over as soon as it felt the shock every time.

I'd like to think that I would have done anything to get myself out of any negative situation. I see myself as a fighter, but I so get why the dog just resigns himself to stay where he is, and that he just takes it after being worn down with life. We lose hope and often believe that it will always be this way, which is why we tend to tell ourselves our "poor me" story.

That this is just how my life is and always will be. Maybe even saying that I'm happy for the people that it works out for, but that's not my life. I think I may have been doing this for years: stuck in my story. I wonder, is that all of us? Have we been conditioned by society, getting shocked along the way, that we forget all that is available to us?

I really believe, now more than ever, that we have the right to be whoever we want to be. We can change at any time. We need collectively to start stepping in that direction and let go of the person we used to be and become the person that we want to be.

The person who's been conditioned vs the person who we truly are. Which hopefully still includes being kind to whoever we meet, with love and respect. Maybe if we live in this way, we won't have to fill ourselves up with things like possessions to make ourselves feel better, which we all know only lasts until the newest version of the latest gadget, or designer clothes come out.

Yesterday I went to see some friends that I hadn't seen in a long time. One of my friends said she had a colonoscopy; she's thirty-five, and as she laid there the doctor said they couldn't find anything, and she said in exasperation, "Are you kidding me," to the doctor, because she had been having stomach problems for a while, and as he was trying to explain it to her.

He said, "Oh wait here's something."

She replied with a, "Thank you," feeling grateful.

I wanted to stop her and say, did you just hear yourself? You want him to find something. You want to be sick, and then he did, and she was. I can't help thinking about all I've been reading and studying lately about intentions. Shouldn't our focus always be on being healthy and happy?

The same thing happened to me the other day, however. I was feeling sad for myself; I had just been to court for the foreclosure of one of my homes. I was very upset, and even more frazzled thinking about my future and how that would look since the attorney hinted to me that this could lead me into bankruptcy.

I called my mom. She's the one person I can sometimes call and talk to when I need a person to share some things with, but when I call her, she often just starts talking and I never get to tell her, or share, or say a word.

This time, I forced my thoughts, worries and fears out as I felt like I really need to be heard, and my mother says to me in my time of great sorrow and need; worried about homelessness, how to make a living now, with utter exhaustion at the thought, *"Who cares, it's over, it's done, blah, blah, blah."*

No really, she said blah, blah, blah, and it's not over, I'm living in it, so I instantly became angry and defensive at the thought of her not caring. Hadn't I been through enough? Then it hit me with my new awareness, *do I really want to argue with her and tell her about all the things that could still go wrong, because I don't want them to happen?*

I used my newfound awareness and believed that she was right. It didn't really feel good at the moment, and I'm not sure that was her intention. Maybe it was, and maybe she could have handled it a little better, but then maybe I wouldn't have gotten it. I need to focus on what I want. What's done is done. I can't change any of that. I just need to move on and start thinking about what I want.

Which, has me wondering about this idea of just switching your thoughts. It's interesting to think that if we don't attach meaning to the words that it's easy to go from the word "*car*" to the word "pizza" to "sunshine." Harder when we say the words "betrayal," "suffering," "happiness." But, aren't they all just words, and isn't it the meaning that we attach to the word that makes us suffer? Why do we let ourselves stay in the suffering when it's all just going on in our heads?

I believe this is where many of us get stuck when we're in that dialog in our mind. We attach all sorts of feelings and emotions to what we're telling ourselves, or what someone has said to us. Why do we allow ourselves to attach negative emotions to just words? If our thoughts and intentions help us to get to the positive outcome that we want, then we have to remember to continually put out into the world that what we want. We can't sit in the unhappiness, unless that's where we want to stay.

Yoga and Meditation Practice

Journal Entry

I'm feeling really good. I'm only thinking of myself and my children right now. I think my children are going to be great! And, for that I'm extremely grateful. All I seem to want to do right now is write, have thoughts, then write some more. I need to run upstairs and pay some bills, but I sit down and write.

I had this thought while practicing yoga this morning. Along the lines of the Goldilocks story of although we are similar, we are also very different and how this relates to everything we do. Which I believe yoga helps us with. What works for one person may not work for another, and we all need to find our own way.

I was just thinking about our bodies, for instance, if you give my blood type to someone it could kill them. To others it can save their lives. What brings me joy, may not be what brings someone else joy.

When I would go visit my grandmother she would try and make me happy and comfortable. She would fix me a special meal that she loved, but I didn't. When I would sit down, she would bring me a pillow and force it behind my head, insisting that now I was more comfortable, but I wasn't. She meant well, but I must remember - be my own guru, and do what's right for me.

And, it's funny the more I practice yoga, the more I have awareness and some form of insight. I'm realizing how many people, like I was and often still am, are just stuck in their own little worlds. Now, I just want to go around shaking everyone, shouting - WAKE UP!

Blog Post - Surrender to the divine all around you.

It's hard to break away from patterns of anything that we're doing... right or wrong. It's hard to change a pattern. Sometimes we are forced to change because of our circumstances. Sometimes we sabotage ourselves from making the change we want, because we are afraid to go forward, and other times it's our fear that brings us closer to what we don't want because that's all we are focusing on.

I am trying to make changes and I'm finding it hard. Sometimes I waver back and forth wondering if I'm doing the right thing. It may

DONNA MELANSON

be because of all the energy and sacrifice that it took to create what life I have now, makes it hard to let go. But I want to pull the band-aid so to speak because I just cannot continue to work in real estate and keep my sanity. It, however, is my only possible income which is a hard factor to overlook.

I'm concerned about spending time and money on my blog, but the thought of not doing it makes me feel like my heart is breaking even more. It seems that if I don't do this, life would be unbearable. Doing it makes me excited and hopeful, but also a little reckless at this time in our economy and in my life where future income is an unknown factor.

Money should be saved for food, and in not doing it, it leaves me in that self-defeating downward spiral with no hope and no happiness. Which I believe will continue to lead me to the life experiences that I do not want.

My original reason for writing the blog besides needing some place to see good in the world was to get me writing. To help me communicate with others. To feel heard, and to keep myself pumped up with positive words. I had felt myself slipping into a deep depression that I needed to get out of. I wanted to feel like someone is listening. I wanted to have hope.

So, I guess I'm going to continue this Goldilocks experiment of having a perfect life and living it in a perfect world. I will not be pushed by my fear! I will be led by my dreams, and I hope you do the same.

Just a thought!
Love, Goldi

Yoga and Meditation Practice

Journal Entry

I've been sitting in the space of awareness for a while wondering why I haven't told everyone about my blog. I think it is because they may think I'm crazy. I've done so many things and I reinvented myself so many times but as I write this, I am realizing that I may not care.

No one in my office knows what I'm going through. I keep showing up, playing the part. They most likely believe, because they know I have land and a house to sell, that I must have money somewhere. I need to start trying to be who I want to become or who it is that I really am. It may be time to share, at least about my book.

Today I told a real estate agent in the office, about the book, and he's already bringing me down. He says, "There's no money in writing a book, what else are you going to do?" I got down for a minute and then started arguing back with him why I wanted to write it, and he just kept popping my bubble.

Another real estate agent walked in and must have heard us, he looked at me and said, *"You're good enough, you're smart enough, and doggone it, people like you,"* with a smile on his face using Saturday Night Live's fictional characters Stuart Smalley's iconic words of positive affirmations, just trying to lift the mood.

I feel like it's something I have to do no matter what, and if it doesn't get published then so be it. Right now, I just need to get it written. It's this internal drive within me compelling me to do it. I think it's possible that the journey is also simply in the doing, that it could bring me to where I want to be.

It sounds silly to some, that's possibly another reason why I don't talk about it. Plus, I've spent my whole life taking care of people, making a whole lot of money, and now since I'm losing it all, I've come to the realization that it didn't make me happy anyway.

Why should I continue living a life that doesn't make me happy? Shouldn't I try to do something different this time around? So, I'm going to focus on a new way of living life. I'm trusting my instincts and doing what I feel I have to do from this place inside, which is what I feel I should have done a long time ago.

This inspiration of doing things differently reminds me of a story I heard at a real estate seminar about a fly at a windowpane that tries desperately to get out of a room. He knows that he has to persevere for his freedom, and he's determined and works hard to get out.

The fly never stops to pause, he keeps going, working harder and harder to get out. The fly never notices that on the other side of the room that there's a window open that would lead him outside, and so the fly often dies.

It sounds like a familiar story. Much like my story if I keep living the way I have, or remembering the story about the dog, conditioned or not, I think possibly we've all been living with blinders on. If our lives are not working in the way we're approaching it, shouldn't we change our process?

Blog Post

An Example of Why Living Your "Just Right" Life Will Not Only Help You but Will Help Heal the World.

Today I woke up in a good mood. I had cleaning to do but I was joyfully cleaning while listening to music. Then I started wondering if my twenty-year-old son was going to come over to mow. It had been two weeks and we've had an unusual amount of rain, so it needed it. I decided to call, and I realized as we talked, that he hadn't even thought about mowing, but said he would figure it out.

About an hour later he called back in an angry resentful voice and said, "Is it raining there, because it's raining here, and I don't want to drive all the way out there if it's going to rain. There's nothing I hate more than mowing in the rain." I immediately got defensive, feeling like I've given him the opportunity to earn money, and selling his services to two other neighbors. And when I got off the phone my mind started racing through other things that made me mad. When all of a sudden, I said wait. This is not the day that I want. What happened and how can I turn this around?

Before I would have been telling myself the story...that here I am trying to do him a favor, and now having the awareness that he may be thinking he's doing me a favor, and by doing something out of obligation he feels resentful, and now so have I. In fact, I've been doing to him what people have been doing to me. So, instead of me trying to help him in this way, it would have been better if I would have supported him in finding his own way. He probably would have chosen something that he enjoyed, or at least felt grateful for. Instead we both we're angry.

In the past I would have continued to be angry the whole day, and it would have affected everyone I came in contact with, and then the anger would have grown as they became affected. So instead, I gave myself an attitude adjustment, and thanked him for coming.

I told him that the next mow would probably be the last for the season, and then to tell everyone that it would be his last year mowing - that he needs to find what brings him joy. He agreed, and said that he told himself that last year, but then he still mowed another year, which confirmed to me why he was resentful.

I hope you get where I'm trying to lead you, that when we do what our heart is calling us to do, we bring joy into our lives and the lives of those around us. The joy grows and that's what we really want... and that's what's best for the world.

Just a thought,
Love, Goldi

Yoga and Meditation Practice

Journal Entry

The Greek philosopher Epictetus said, "If you want to improve, be content to be thought foolish and stupid." My therapist told me today that he had a client that wanted to become an actress but decided not to because she knew that she would not like the paparazzi. Suggesting that she was putting the cart before the horse, which was keeping her from moving forward - the fear of what may come.

I don't want to stop trying. Who knows what the future holds? Write, write, write, and post!

Journal Entry and Positive Statement, Using the prompt - What will they say ten years from now?

Here I'm envisioning what I want people to say about me, and what I would want to say about myself, ten years from now.

Please remember, no laughing, well you can if you want.

Circa 2009 - Looking Forward

Donna Melanson - battled her way through life, fighting, and unhappy, until she finally learned her lesson and relaxed into life. She has spent the last ten years preaching this message on how to have a happy life. Finding peace within, without further ado here she is...

I am so happy and grateful that I'm here before you today. Living my perfect life of writing, traveling, and spreading the message of joy and how to live your perfect life.,

I want to practice a little self-love and congratulate myself for finally waking up and learning how to have the happiness that I've sought. I love my life and I do things that make me happy, it feels effortless.

When I was a freshman in college. I wanted to do so well. I studied so hard and ended up on academic probation. I kind of gave up in a way. Wrong words, I relaxed, and let go of the outcome. I still studied hard but didn't worry, but just did the best that I could. I didn't get straight A's, but I did get out of my academic probation and I did go on to graduate.

That's what happened to me later on in life. I wanted to succeed so bad that I kept forcing myself to do the things that I didn't want to do in a suffering way. It's why I had stomach problems, resentment, and unhappiness. I think there are many ways to succeed, and we do need to make an effort, but we need to think of a way that feels right to us. It will be authentic, and it will feel effortless. Even though it won't be effortless, we're not going to be just sitting on the couch, wishing, without doing anything. Our minds will be in the right place, while we're actively taking steps, towards our goal.

When I started out, I wanted to be a writer, traveler, meet great people, have great friends, and relationships, eat delicious healthy foods and be in great shape. I pictured this glamorous lifestyle of happiness. So, when I was losing everything, I started writing in my vinyl sided house that I use to rent out that was in the flight path of the airport, with views of the power plant. I started practicing yoga at home and went with a friend for a walk twice a week for 30 minutes at a local park. I started cooking healthier foods, now that I could no longer afford to go out to eat. Then I realized hey, in a way, I'm living my perfect life already. So, I just kept doing that until it became more of what I wanted. It wasn't entirely what I was envisioning, but the essence of what I wanted was. It started from knowing what I wanted, and then living the actions of the life that I wanted.

Blog Post - Fill the negative with the positive!

Today's reminder: If I am sad, I will deliberately cultivate some happy thoughts. If I am judging someone or something, I will look for the good, and fix my mind on that. If I am doubtful that my life will turn around, I will look for all the good that I already have. If I am lonely, I will reach out and be a friend.

Let's dig all of those negative thoughts out of our body, mind and soul, in our feelings, actions and words, and make a conscious effort to fill up and seek out the positive in everything we say, do, and feel!

Just a thought!
Love, Goldi
Goldilocks Blog
Searching for the Perfect Life in a Perfect World

Blog Post

You are capable of so much. Have the courage to do something different, to adapt and change! In whatever you decide, if it's what you want to do, talk about it. Step up and step out! Be noticed! Try new things and expect more.

Just a thought!
Love, Goldi
Goldilocks Blog
Searching for a perfect life in a perfect world...

Yoga and Meditation Practice

Journal Entry – I'm so Lucky!

The world works in mysterious ways sometimes, and often we don't know how lucky we really are. Today, I saw an old co-worker, a real estate agent, and reluctantly I spoke to her. I'm embarrassed because all of my properties are listed and this is a small town, and everyone knows my business. Sometimes I think people enjoy watching people fail. Anyway, we exchanged pleasantries and then I asked the question that I had been afraid, for my egos stake, to ask. "Are you enjoying living in the downtown condo?" The condo was a real estate deal that we both had invested in.

I had to bow out of the deal, not so gracefully, for obvious financial reasons, about a year ago. I needed my twenty-five thousand back to live on. It was a deal, however, so great that even in this economic storm that we're still in, is still sound. Devastated and embarrassed, I awaited her answer. I was surprised, when she let me know that she also had to run away from the deal.

She then proceeded to tell me that I was the only person who got to walk away with the money that they'd invested. I had no idea that I was so lucky. My children and I would not have been able to eat or pay my bills without those funds. I had been grateful that I had received the money, but now it has me wondering - what other lucky blessings, have I missed?

Yoga and Meditation Practice

Journal Entry

The windows of my home are open, and I see a low flying airplane getting ready to land. I hear the rush of cars and trucks, horns and sirens on the interstate nearby. My view as I peer out includes three tall towers with steam pouring out, courtesy of the local power plant that also has a certain and distinct smell. Today it's combined with a neighbor burning a not so pleasant mixture of wood and plastic. I turn my attention, so that I don't get too involved, and focus instead on the beauty of the oak, maple and poplar trees that frame the vision of the power plant, and the cute little white daisies in the sea foam green ceramic pot that I planted last spring. All reminding me of how grateful I am to have a roof over my head.

Yoga and Meditation Practice

Journal Entry

Okay so I guess if I'm going to do this, meaning write, there are a few things I need to do like start packing and selling items to sustain us. Plan on writing daily. I need to be better. I need to work harder on my work, my cleaning, my organization. I'm going to focus only on the life that I want for me and my children. Exercise! Keep planning for myself and let it grow! Let the desire build up and bubble out. Think success! Think joy! Think happiness! Visualize the trip and the journey! Visualize Max and Ally being happy and successful in their own way! Thinking back to that motto of the 70's, that I can be whatever I want! Visualize the perfect man and family.

Positive statement set in the present tense - I'm so grateful now that my children are happy and healthy, I am writing and traveling and I'm capturing it all with video and photos of all the most beautiful places, the most beautiful things, and the most beautiful and inspiring people that I see and meet. I'm grateful for my perfect health and that I keep looking younger and younger. I am beautiful inside and out. I help others through my blog through the words given to me from a higher source. Grateful for the right people and opportunities that come my way. I am so blessed.

Positive statement set in the present tense - I'm so grateful now that I see myself in my new home. I love that the house is filled with bright sunshine coming in through the windows all day long. The large windows that look out over the majestic blue ridge mountains. I love walking outside, taking a deep breath, as I do a half sun salutation by raising my arms as I breathe in, forward folding as I lower my arms to the earth while exhaling. I then lift halfway up as I inhale only to exhale and forward fold again, before inhaling my arms all the way up as I stand back up then lowering my arms back to the heart center. And as I do this, I'm thanking God for this most beautiful day!

I see and feel myself here truly with gratitude for all I've been given. For the gifts of love, joy, happiness and divine grace. I feel this love and favor coming from this higher source, as I mentally walk back into my home. I twirl about with outstretched arms, taking in all that's been given to me.

Positive statement set in the present tense - I'm so grateful for my life. I see myself in my mind with my imagination, going into the family room area to sit down at my computer. I take one deep breath as I open my computer to write and to plan my next trip. My husband comes to greet me as he lovingly greets me with a kiss on my cheek. I love him so much. I am truly blessed.

I am so happy and grateful that I have money coming in from multiple sources, and that I have someone that I trust handling that for me. I'm grateful that I'm healthy and that I even feel healthier every day. I eat well and I joyfully exercise.

Yoga and Meditation Practice

Journal Entry

Ally and I went to visit a college for an interview for a scholarship based on merit and financial need. Soon we will have nothing. She's dreamed of becoming a doctor, and I've never seen anyone work so hard and handle so much.

I've moved her and her brother every two years, fixing homes up and then selling them. All the while they were also alternating back and forth to their father's house every other week for pretty much all of their childhood. Dealing with father, stepmother, step siblings, each other and me, affected by all of our stuff, and simply being teenagers.

She has volunteered, worked, played soccer, and still managed to graduate at the top of her class. I write this about her because as we sit here in the restaurant, everyone is casual, nice and friendly, but you can sense an air of wealth. I think, definitely, a whole other level to where we've been, not a snobby show off wealth but just a sense that they are there and have no worries of money.

I never felt like that and wonder if maybe this is why I am where I am today, they seem extremely happy and strangely calm. Ally must feel it too because all of a sudden, she blurts out that she no longer feels guilty anymore if she were to win this scholarship.

I understand where she's coming from, we've had more than enough for a while, so it seems awkward and odd to now need to seek help for her to go to college. But my mind keeps coming back to this feeling. I've never felt this energy before, it's hard to describe other than there was an air about the environment we were in.

It and the people in it felt grounded and happy but not overly, but at the same time happy at a higher different level. As if, they knew definitively that the universe was working for them, so they didn't have to worry.

I think I've always had the feeling like I didn't have enough, I needed to work harder, and it's probably why I'm where I am, with only the satisfaction of trying to do my best. Now I'm just hoping that I can keep a roof over Ally's head until she graduates and hope to figure out how to tap into this energy. I believe that I'm missing something.

Yoga and Meditation Practice

Journal Entry

Daily, I cannot wait to get up in the morning and start writing after I practice a little yoga and meditation. I can't believe how good it makes me feel with clarity and purpose. I really feel happy, and I'm not worrying as much anymore about my former life, and what's been lost. I'm going to do what makes me happy today. I've lived too long in that other world, in that other reality. No more suffering, I want happiness!

People have been telling me lately that they can see it in my face and hear it in my voice. So, I'm going to sit here in my house every morning and remember to keep in mind to continue the dream and visualize my perfect life. To be grateful for all I have right now. For all of my experiences as they have brought me a true depth and knowing of how these things work.

I'm loving life now, there is so much beauty to see. This is my time, to write, to feel full of life, and to take it all in. I write my journal entries, my positive statement. Right now, I'm saying to myself, Money comes easily to me, and I'm receiving it, knowing that I deserve it. We all do. Every human being on this earth deserves to have health, wealth and happiness. I want that's for all!

Blog Entry - Gratitude

The traditional Thanksgiving Day has come and gone, but it makes me think. Shouldn't we celebrate it every day? Studies have shown that people who are grateful have higher levels of well-being. They tend to be happier, more satisfied, develop self-acceptance and a purpose in their lives. They sleep better and cope better with positive thoughts and actions. Life just tends to be better. And, I'm all for that!

So, cheers to celebrating Thanksgiving each and every day!
Just a thought!
Love, Goldi
GoldilocksBlog.com
No longer searching but having a perfect life in a perfect world.

Yoga and Meditation Practice

Journal Entry / Positive Statement

(Here I'm trying to really shift my energy, as I write about the life I want to live.)

I am so happy and grateful, I am so happy and grateful, I am so happy and grateful, I AM SO HAPPY AND GRATEFUL, I REALLY AM SO HAPPY AND GRATEFUL FOR EVERYTHING! Thank God, Thank God, Thank God! I guess God knew I would be so stubborn that he would have to continually bring me to my knees to get me to wake up.

I'm so grateful for my past because I would not have been able to get to this point without all the failure. If it had not been for the complete failure. I would not have looked at my life with such introspection. I would not have looked for ways to live life differently. I would not have deeply known the real me. The real me is an introvert, quiet, and kind. The real me is compelled to see the good in all. The real me wants to help others see the good that I see.

I would, however, have liked to not suffer so much, but apparently, I needed to, or it wouldn't have come to this. I mean it would have been nice to have the money and conveniences that I had grown accustomed to and be a being of peace that gives to all, but that's not what needed to happen.

I have however, such hope and faith for my future. I don't know what will happen, but I know it will be for the best. I keep embracing my happiness, and envisioning my perfect life in the future, with gratitude for the life I have now. I love my life. I love my house. I love my cars. I love this view. I love the people I meet. I love the places I will go. I love the new ideas I have on living the perfect life for ourselves and the whole. I love making one small step in a positive direction, or speaking a kind word, that leaves a ripple effect of good.

Good things are happening all the time for me and my family. It's as if I've taken a step into heaven on earth. I love my life. I'm going to close my eyes now and envision and feel gratitude for all the things I have now.

Yoga and Meditation Practice

Journal Entry - December 1, 2009

Well, I felt really good about giving my notice, and yet here I am at the real estate office, wondering why I'm here. Is it because old habits are hard to break, or am I still hedging my bets? When am I ever going to learn? I've told my boss already, but he told me to think about it, which I have. I've thought long and hard about it. This feels like I'm wasting my time, but I'm trying to go with the flow and not fight it.

Who knows what this is going to bring - maybe it's part of the larger plan? I'm trying to take care of myself after all of the years of neglect. But this awareness of letting go of the outcome reminds me of a story that I'm not sure I can adequately tell or remember. But it goes something like this.

Once upon a time, there were two magical elves who were looking for a place to sleep for two nights. The first house they came to was a large mansion with an iron gate and a long winding driveway that circled in front of the house. They knocked on the door of this home and asked for shelter and food for the night. The owner looked down at them and said dinner time is over, but you can go to the basement for the night.

When they arrived at the bottom of the stairs to the basement, all they saw was a room devoid of anything but a hard floor. But they were grateful for the shelter. The younger elf noticed later that the older elf began patching a hole in the wall before they fell asleep. Then in the morning they were asked to leave.

Upon searching for shelter and food, the next night the two elves arrived at a small one room house. As the elves stepped on the porch, they could hear the people inside and smell a stew cooking on the stove. Upon knocking on the door, the husband and wife let them in. They were just sitting down to eat and shared with the elves the food that they had made, enough just for themselves.

When it was time to go to sleep, they made the elves as comfortable as they could, and in the morning when they woke up, they could hear the anguish of the farmer who just came in the house upset that his only cow had just died. The young elf looked at the older elf with anger and said; *We came to the first house, and the people were not kind and yet you repaired their wall, and here the people have been so kind and generous to us and yet you let their only cow die.*

The older elf then explained to the younger elf that when he saw the hole in the wall, he peered into it and saw that it was filled with gold, so he it patched up. And, last night when the angel of death came, he came for the farmer's wife, and he gave him the cow instead. Silent, the young elf understood.

Sometimes when we think things are bad, it may not be as bad as it could have been. Have faith. I'm trying to remind myself of that as I get a phone call from another real estate agent asking me about my personal home that went into foreclosure. Saying that they hated to call but they needed more information.

I'm feeling like I'm being gut punched again, a continuing repeated occurrence in my adult life. This is about the ninth time I have had agents call me about it. Every time I've been caught off guard, since I've been trying to change my mindset. I need to figure out a way to handle these blows. I just don't feel so great after being reminded of my foreclosed home… more humility, more humble pie to eat.

I do remember and try to use all of my newfound positive gumption to remind myself that I'm going to be okay. I'm actually even feeling it on a relationship level. Last night Alan sent me a plane ticket to fly out to LA.

Out of the blue he just sent me a text and asked if I wanted to come, and since I do want to travel more, and my mom just happens to be in town so she and Ally can look after each other. Going with the flow, I said "Yeah maybe, send me some details."

He said he would, but then around 5:30, I received a text to check my email. He had sent a plane ticket to leave this Thursday and fly back on Tuesday. So, I guess I'm going. I feel a little crazy for going after "closing the book" and all, but I'm going to go with the flow.

At the office I get an email from Nick, a lawyer in town, that I went to college with. He's really handsome, and a really good guy. We went out once on a Saturday afternoon, for a short hike next to a picturesque river, and then had a drink at a local pub. I thought we were having a really good time when he said he had to leave because his mother and his aunt were expecting him home for dinner. I disappointedly drove home and that was it. His email is saying that we need to go out for another beer. I told him I was going out of town this weekend but could use a drink now.

I know Nick works downtown too and I think a beer could really help soften the blow of that phone call that I just took asking me about my home, while I'm here sitting at the office, surrounded by the other real estate agents.

He wrote back IPA or dark? I wrote back dark of course, my favorite, but that was it. No response back. I secretly hoped he would show up, but I guess I will take the compliment right now that at least he was thinking of me. Some interest is good.

Blog Post - Attitude

I remind myself that I'm in charge of my attitude, and I finally realize the impact of attitude on my life. I've always believed the expression of "Whether you think you can, or can't, you're right," but I think I may need to implement that more.

I've noticed in others the self-defeating attitude that many have. In fact, it's one of my many pet peeves, hearing people complain about something and not doing anything about it, and I admit that I've been guilty of that myself. I believe attitude is more important than what we think are the facts.

It's more important than what's happened in our past. It's more important than what we've succeeded and failed in; more important than the amount of education that we have, or the amount of money in our bank account. It's even more important than our gifts and skills.

If we focus on what is good in our lives, what is joyful, what is possible, and what it is we want, ... If we believe and take the steps to get where we want to go, we get to at least, have the satisfaction of moving towards our perfect life now.

Just a thought!
Love, Goldi
GoldilocksBlog.com
Having the perfect life in a perfect world...

Yoga and Meditation Practice

Journal Entry

My trip to see Alan wasn't any different than any other time I've gone to see him. I was there with him, but he wasn't with me. We went to a golf tournament where he was coaching. I found myself walking sometimes with the player's girlfriend and often alone. In the players' clubhouse that's only available for players, their families, and the caddies, at the end of the day, I sat and ate with everyone but after, coach and players disappeared to a private room. I sat at the table alone as everyone else at the table knew people at the other tables.

The next day he got up early to work out his player before the next round, and after, he coached some players while I sat alone in the hotel room. So, no, nothing had changed with Alan or me, I don't know why we bother, but it's upset me because I'm always hopeful, this time will be different. I need to remember that I've already know how this book ends. I guess on the positive side, I did have the experience of being at a big golf tournament and got to see what it looks like behind the scenes.

My dad called me twice yesterday, like he was panicking, or irritated, or maybe just wanting to rub it in that loan service agents are calling him about payments on my loan, which just adds more salt to my wounds. Another humiliating experience - yay me. I received the call while just finishing up showing houses with one of my coworkers, so I felt the need to explain, and I went on to tell her more of my story than she probably wanted to know.

Embarrassed but feeling a little blank, I told her many of my

DONNA MELANSON

mistakes, and of the life I was trying to create. I'm surprised, that she doesn't think I'm crazy. Every time I tell someone that I want to write and travel, and they act like I'm sane and that I can do it... It blows my mind. Maybe these are the type of people I need to surround myself with.

To my rational mind it seems like a pipe dream that many people have. But I do have this burning desire that it's something that I have to do, no matter what. Maybe not believing is where I go wrong. I'm growing more confident every day. Crazy, but loving it.

Talked to Sam the other day, you know my friend who puts me away with his fishing poles, and my conversation with him blew my mind. First of all, since we only ever saw each other about a few times a year, I've told him that I wasn't going to keep having, the same type of relationship with him. Now, he's become super attentive.

Well, I guess it's Sam, I should say more attentive, which seems super attentive coming from him. We've been video chatting. I guess I'm just lonely which is probably why I've hung out with him for so long. He's just the one and only person that's been kind of around and I do enjoy my time spent with him, and now that we're video chatting, I see love and desire in his eyes like he wants to jump through the screen and devour me.

But, in our conversations he says things like "I don't know if I've ever loved or what it feels like, or if I ever will." "We're just two souls who found each other." I'm so confused by this, but I've learned over the years that you have to believe people when they tell you something like that. It's usually a warning, and the truth. So, I take him at his word.

Tonight, as my friend, I told him about Alan, and asked him

if that made him feel relieved, that I'm not holding on to him. I never could put my finger on why he stayed away and had maybe falsely assumed it was because he thought I wanted him too much or something. It's interesting all the stories we can make up about something when we don't really know the answer. He answered me by saying, "I just never let the green man of envy get to me." Which wasn't really what I was talking about, since I didn't think he cared in the first place.

As a woman, it's hard for us to sometimes "just date," and it's even harder when you live in different cities, but for some reason we've both just kept it quiet about each other for whatever reasons. But when a man tells you that he doesn't want to be your boyfriend and you come to fully realize this, it kind of hits you at your core. Then when they say they never want to stop seeing you, it becomes really confusing and very much reminding me of my ex-husband who wanted to have his cake and eat it too.

But I want it all now, and I'm not settling for anything or anyone who is not the best for me. My "perfect life" that I'm trying to create as I write my Goldilocks blog and positive statements in the present tense in my journal entries, does not read and I saw him maybe once a month and never introduced him to my family. No, my "perfect life" has a fully committed perfect man, fully invested in my family. I don't want parts of a few men that I balance together to give me one perfect man. *No*, I want *the* perfect man for me and only me!

Oh, but I started off telling you about what blew my mind today with my conversation with Sam, as I was opening up to him about everything. I told him that for whatever reason my heart had been with him, and that I finally can let it move away, and then he did something that I was shocked to see.

He moved his body forward bending at the hips, and then began

DONNA MELANSON

rocking back and forth as if he wanted to get up and go, or comfort himself, or shake it off, while he was saying, "Wow that's deep," and it looked almost like he would cry. Like he had a heart. Like I hurt him. I couldn't believe it. I just thought that he was being a dude and that I was not exactly what he wanted, or I felt he would have made room for me in his life.

Now I'm thinking wow what happened in his life that made him this way? Does this mean he cares? Do I even care now - is it too late? Maybe it was just a moment for him. I don't know. What I do know now more than ever, is that we all must do our own work.

Positive Statement Set in the Present Tense

I'm so grateful now that I have the money for everything that I need and want. Money comes to me easily from positive and happy sources. My children are happy, healthy and they are living their perfect lives. I'm happy that I can travel to anywhere I want. I have the love of a great man who is dedicated to me, who loves me with all of his heart, who is kind and considerate and thoughtful.

I respect him and I'm so happy that he's so capable of handling so many things for me. We make our lives together full and for both our benefit. I'm grateful that I followed my dream, that it's successful and that it's helped other people. I love my home. I love where I live. I love being with my family. I love the people I meet and the people I get reacquainted with. I love my life!

Yoga and Meditation Practice

Journal Entry

I just heard from Nick; you know the good-looking attorney who asked me about the bar tour but then never messaged me again. We went to the same college, and I met him at the gym after my divorce and then again among friends at my college homecoming years ago. After the homecoming get together, we went out that one time for a hike and a drink one afternoon.

He's so good looking, tall, dark, handsome, and a perfect gentleman. He's an ex-marine, lawyer, loves the outdoors and cares about the earth and all people on it. Not sure at all what his deal is though, he's a complete mystery. But since he reached out to me again, and I just read my email about the holiday commercial Real Estate party, I thought it would be nice to show up for once with someone, before I finally pull the plug and get out of this business altogether. I've been going to these events solo for years.

I have no idea what people think of me, but I often get looks from the women if I go to speak to the men who I associate with, and if I don't go talk to them, then I'm just sitting alone. Plus, it may help him since he's starting a new practice in town, and, it will get me out of the house. So, I asked him if he would go with me, and surprisingly he said yes.

I was excited finally to RSVP plus one. However, he just called an hour and a half before the event was about to start and said that he was doing his Marines Toys for Tots event and they were asking him to bring the money downtown after, so he thought it would push him too late and so he wouldn't be able to go with me after all.

I'm unfortunately used to men not being there for me, but I hear my voice quivering as I tell him that it's okay. He says I should go anyway, and I tell him that, maybe I will, as I think of how embarrassing it's going to be after finally not RSVPing single to an event, and then showing up without my plus one. That's a new one. I've never done that before.

A few days went by and I had forgotten all about it until Nick emailed me and said how sad he was that he could not go and asked how the event went. I don't get him at all, but I replied truthfully. I said, *I had a great time. At first, I was bummed, since you weren't going with me, and that I was going to have to attend another event alone.*

Especially since I'm getting out of real estate, and since the other members of the group are mostly men, it's usually a little uncomfortable with their wives and such. So, I usually go dressed conservatively, and placate myself by doing what I feel will make the wives comfortable with me, and the men usually ignore me for whatever reason. This time, however, I said "F" it. I dressed a little sexy, with just a hint of conservative flare, and went out full of myself.

I put on my high heel boots which made me taller than most of the men, and I walked in owning the place, and you know what? I had the best time ever. I felt like a celebrity. It was strange. People were going out of their way to talk to me. Finally acting like they know me, like old friends, as they came to talk to me in a group. Which I think made other people want to come and talk to me.

It was so weird. I think for years I played myself down, not wanting to draw too much attention to myself for fear of wrath and retribution from the wives. This time, I think instead of giving me the stink eye or feeling sorry for me, I think they wanted to be me. Man did it feel good. I really did need that ego boost, and I hope I continue to try to always put my best self out there from here on out, and truly just be me.

That was probably way more than what you wanted to hear, but you asked.

I've heard nothing back, laughing out loud, but I think this is how I'm feeling about life. "F" it! I'm going to go out and have a good life. I keep waiting for my man to allow my life to fully begin, but I'm not going to anymore! I'm going to live!

Yoga and Meditation Practice

Journal Entry

I haven't received my payment from Michelle for the car I financed for her a few years ago. I'm grateful now, it pays my electricity and phone, but today's the eighteenth and I still haven't received the payment. She, I'm sure, doesn't know what I'm going through. It's a little ironic though, because I remember her being upset about people who owe her money and then being late with payments and the bad karma that would ensue them, for doing her wrong.

I talked to my private lender today and told him I was getting out of real estate to focus on writing my book, to tell my story about standing back up again. He said I should've slept with him, because that would have made it more interesting.

Positive Statement in the Present Tense

I'm so happy and grateful now that I'm living my happy life. I have a wonderful husband who knows and loves all of me. I have full faith and trust in him. I know him deeply and love all of him. Our children and ourselves are all healthy and happy. I'm living a life of peace and happiness; good things continue to come my way.

Circa Now

In my failures and failed attempts to help many people, I realize that loving people and wanting to help all that I meet become more of who they are, is not a negative like I was beginning to think, but a core part of who I am, and even with all the failed attempts, it's still who I want to be. What I've realized is that I can inspire others, but they have to make their own choices and do their own work, and so do I.

I wish I could say I did not feel bitterness after my failures, but I did. I resented all who I helped. I was wrong, and because of it I suffered. It was my failure that gave me my freedom. It was my failure that led me to seek happiness. It was my failure that made me realize that I did do the right thing in helping others, by believing in them and the greatness that I saw.

If only I believed in the greatness of me. And, maybe in a weird way I did help them, not in the way that I thought I would, but in the way they needed. Just like my failure is helping me live the life I've always wanted. I hope that in any future thoughts of failure or wrongdoing or setbacks, that I'll have enough sense to just take a deep breath in and remind myself that this is all somehow for the best, even though it really sucked living through it. Getting to a place of peace in my body and in my mind, however, and connecting to the true essence of who I am, and embracing it, I believe is priceless and true success.

Forgiveness is for yourself, because all those thoughts of resentment that you are holding on to, are wreaking havoc within your body. Resentment creates a tense body, and over the years this tension accumulates. Muscles tighten and you lose flexibility, not only in your body but in your mind. I know you have felt it, your body tenses just with the thought of trauma, your body tenses when someone walks into a room shouting whether it's at you or not. Some people don't even have to shout.

In truth, they don't even have to be physically present, our thoughts and memories take care of triggering resentment without any physical contact at all. Those feelings are affecting you on every level of your being, and without awareness instead of helping you work through it, they are blocking you from your healing.

So, when you begin to forgive the person, even when the person is yourself, you let all the resentment go, you let all the negativity go, and what happens when you do this, the negative energy is released from your body, and from your mind. So, what you're actually doing, is nurturing, nourishing, and healing yourself.

Forgive and let it go, let it go, let it go. Heal thy self and start believing on every level of your being, that you love yourself enough to give this gift to you. Have this mindset and then you will have the healing you need. Remember to remember, to let it go. Remember to remember, to shift your thoughts, to what you want to focus on that keeps you in the present moment and keeps you moving towards a life living in peace.

The first yoga sutra says yoga begins now, so the awareness of the union of the body and mind must forever be constant. We must practice living in the present moment. Not getting emotionally involved in the story we're telling because it's not happening right now, whether it's something from the past or something we fear for the future. Stay in the moment that you're in.

My first yoga teacher taught me that the easiest way to stay in the present is to come back to the awareness of the breath. Always come back to the breath she said. So, let's take a moment here to practice being in the moment, and the positive effects of focusing on the breath. Begin by being aware of where you are with detached awareness.

Just notice and be a witness as you begin to breathe deeper and fuller, as you continue to breathe deeply and exhaling slowly, noticing the rhythm of the breath, the texture of the breath, the sensation of the breath, aware that you're breathing and alive with energy and vibration.

Taking in good rich energy as you inhale, and with every exhalation just feel yourself releasing a little more, letting go a little more, surrendering a little more to the moment that you're in. Take one more nice long slow deep breath in, holding for just a moment, before slowly letting it all go. Take a moment, to "just be."

The harm in not doing this work for yourself, is that it not only affects you but everyone around you, by your actions and attitude. It affects everyone physically as well as mentally. We have the help of our emotions, that sends us signals alerting us, that something is going on inside both positive and negative. Don't judge yourself, just have awareness, and if you need to, shift your thoughts, then shift your actions.

Learn to let go of your attachments to the story that you've been telling yourself. Let go of the grief. It does not serve you in any way. Everyone that has/will or loves you now, doesn't want you spending your life grieving, they want you living life fully, while you can. They want to grab you by the shoulders and gently shake you, saying wake up, wake up and get up - live fully.

Start living in this awareness because I don't want you wasting a decade or two of your life like I did. Wake up and send love to the people you feel have harmed you. I know it's hard, for years I didn't want to, but I realized I had to so that I could end my suffering. I sent deep love and gratitude, for the benefit of the person I knew I was becoming. No one else could give me that relief but me.

I was the only one who could free me, so I had to do the work and feel the love for myself, and I had to let it go, and so do you. No one else can give you the relief but you. Let it go, let it go, let it go, or continue on like I did, and suffer some more.

Start by paying attention to your thoughts without getting involved in them, by just having awareness. Start learning more about yourself with this awareness. Start shifting your thoughts to all the good you have in your life right now. Have compassion for yourself, you've been through a lot.

And because you know what you've been through, you know that you deserve love. So, love yourself. Be kind to yourself. In fact, take a moment now to honor yourself as the beautiful unique being that you are, just as you are right now!

Do it simply for the pure pleasure of doing so.

Yoga and Meditation Practice

Journal Entry

I think it's funny, today is Christmas and I'm sitting here alone again, but this time I'm happy. Maybe it's because I have five men who've texted me, wishing me a Merry Christmas. It's flattering, but like I said funny, because like I said for the millionth time, I'm sitting home alone which I have been for 99% of my nights for the last ten years.

This year I have Ally with me full time, but Max and she are at their dads right now. I'm just really kind of amused because I've cried myself asleep so many nights in the last twenty years being alone, the majority of my adult life. Alone in my marriage. Alone being single. Miserable in both.

Now after much work on myself, it seems like out of the blue and overnight I feel happy. Is this why these men are reaching out to me? They sense this happiness out in the universe – maybe, but whatever it is, I know I'm not going to settle for anything but the best. I'm finally loving myself.

Blog Post

New Year – New Life

Today's the first day of the greatest year ever! Decide today what your perfect life looks like this year, keep this image in mind all year long and allow yourself to make the journey! This may require some courage, which is not necessarily moving forward without fear, but the ability to step into who you are becoming. Who you are at your soul level?

Feel the feeling of gratitude and abundance in your heart, in whatever task you do, each and every day, all year long. Always keeping in mind what your perfect life looks like.

My mantra for this year is; Living Large and Thinking Big! Feeling a huge increase in love, health, wealth, travel, with time for creative writing, while inspiring others towards their happy and perfect lives.

With Love and Gratitude to you this New Year!
Goldi
Having a perfect life in a perfect world!

Blog Post Goldilocks Blog

Years ago, I stayed in the beautiful Mandarin Oriental Hotel, Hyde Par, London. In my room the stereo was turned on, and as I was walking into a room the radio station personality was posting this question to his audience. "What would you do if you only had one day to change your life?"

Yesterday I asked my friend this question, and her response was, "I think that's the problem that we think we only have one day." Hmmm, she's right I thought, it's very true that every day we have an opportunity to start again, or make steps towards our goals, but isn't it a luxury to think that we have forever?

I found this question while perusing through my old journal entries, along with my answer that I wanted to travel and write. I had let ten years go by before I started writing and didn't even realize it. How lucky am I to have another day? I have to say that the entry did also make me feel a little saner, reconfirming, that my desire to write and travel is not just a passing whim, but something deep seated within me.

My point is, I messed up. I wrote down what I wanted to do. I wrote down what I wanted my life to look like, but I didn't do anything to make that happen, not that day or the day after. So, what can you do today, big or small, that will lead you toward your perfect life?

Just a thought!
Love, Goldi
Having a perfect life in a perfect world.

Goldilocks Blog Post – Self Love

No one knows what you're feeling. Sometimes, you don't even know, but instead it manifests in aches and stomach upset, anxiety or depression. At times like this you need to treat and care for yourself as you would a small child, doing whatever it takes to make yourself stronger.

Only you know what it will take. Have fun, meditate, exercise or do whatever it is that brings you joy and peace. Connecting with your true essence will fill yourself blissfully with love. It may feel a little selfish, but remember, we are all connected, and moving into a higher vibration not only helps you, but it elevates those around you. It helps us all!

Just a thought!
Love, Goldi
GoldilocksBlog.com
Having a perfect life in a perfect world...

Yoga and Meditation Practice

Journal Entry

Thinking of my vitamin store today and how the young men that ran the store could take the same supplements and have different results, despite living in the same area, the same environment, being the same height, weight, age and race. What worked for one of them didn't work for the other one.

They both would swear by different products, which makes me think of the Goldilocks fairy tale story and why we should never think that there is just one ideal. The Goldilocks principle should be fluid and different for each individual. Goldilocks was looking for perfect everything, and the bears each had their perfect everything. None of them being right for the other.

So, we must remember that our perfect life may not look like anyone else's in the world, and that's okay, as long as we're not hurting anyone or anything.

We need to have this awareness in everything we do – no judgements. We need to be allowed and expected to change and evolve and adapt as we gain more knowledge and awareness.

Every day that I write my positive statement I envision myself living that life, and I embody the feelings of love and happiness. I see myself sitting on a white sand beach just like the white sand shown in my yoga video that I've been watching daily. I sense that I'm blissfully happy there in a way that I've often been jealous about. And, while I'm thinking and writing about it, I really feel it. I really believe, and I don't know where this belief is coming from, but I believe this practice is changing my life.

Nothing is selling in real estate; I don't qualify for any help and my only income now is one hundred dollars a week that I get from cleaning a law office one day a week. A friend of mine hooked me up with this gig, and I'm so grateful. I've felt such a weight of what I've been going through that some days I just can't seem to manage anything else. Ally and I, however, need to eat. Luckily, Max has been living on his own for quite some time and doing well enough. I believe he'll be okay.

Positive Statement Set in the Present Tense

I'm so grateful that I started living the life that I wanted and that I'm now financially successful with money coming to me from several sources. I'm grateful to be living with the man that I'll spend the rest of my life with, full of love and support. We're both living fulfilling lives.

We write our own story, where we each pursue our dreams apart and our dreams together. I'm happy and healthy living my perfect life – thinking as I write, smiling that, *out of manure, comes flowers.*

Yoga and Meditation Practice

Journal Entry

My self-defeating mantra is, "The only common denominator in my troubles, is me." I did not sleep well last night; I've always wanted my memoir to have a happy ending. I wanted to show that somehow, I came through the sadness and was able to travel to all the happiest places in the world and write about it. But a friend that I've shared this with just gave me a book where the writer did just that.

It was published the same month I started my blog. It's made me seriously sad like I've been gut punched again. I'm having my own little pity party. The book is even on the best sellers list. My daughter tries to cheer me up and says that people interested in that subject always want to know more. Which is true, I believe, but I'm at the moment diving deep into despair.

My goal, in reality, was that as soon as I took my daughter to college this August that I would somehow travel and write, searching for all the happiest places in the world. I've been making plans, packing up belongings, and organizing my life to leave. I try to blog about things that I want to remember to pump myself up. Just knowing that I would soon be off and on my journey. That's what's kept me going.

The oddest thing is that the book has several similarities to me, mentioning South Florida, North Carolina and Bhutan, which is one of the first place that I wanted to go... now I'm laughing, crying, and feeling foolish with busted balloons, spilled milk and there is no Santa Claus kind of feeling.

Yoga and Meditation Practice

Journal Entry

I seriously believe my dream is done after finding out about Erick Weiner's new book. I need a way to make money. I guess this is a sign. I'm really pissed. I'm in such a bad mood. And, then I talked to a dear old friend today who told me that things with her, were not that good. They couldn't go to Breckinridge Colorado this year, because finances were tight. But they still have two homes, a boat and plane.

They've also had to recently adjust and go to church on another night so that they didn't have to split time between the church and the club, and the poor thing had to cut her housekeeper back to three days a week. I really hate it for her. She said at least I did something with my life, she just gave her life to her family.

Which upset me even more, but I hope I didn't show it because I love her madly. She's been such a good friend to me, and she really doesn't mean anything bad by it. It's her story. But since I'm feeling sorry for myself today it really pisses me off, because I feel I also gave my whole life to my family. Everything I did was to make my children's life better.

I had to be mom and dad. With no support for myself, no one

DONNA MELANSON

to share the burdens, and with no time for fun. I don't even have the luxury to have a breakdown, although I guess I should be glad about that. Fuck that shit. I guess her pain is real. I guess everyone's pain is real.

I guess, embarrassingly, we don't really know what the pain someone else is going through. And, comparatively, I need to remember that someone out there is going through, and has been through, way, way, way, worse stuff than me.

Yikes – a thought just popped into my head. I don't know where it came from, but it just asked if I was going to use this as an excuse to quit. Thinking maybe, but if I do, I'm the only one who loses. I guess, I know, I'm still going to write my memoir.

That thought never really left me, but where's my happy ending? I'll try and let it all slide and believe and have faith that the universe is working for my benefit, and that somehow, all of this is a blessing.

Positive Statement Set in the Present Tense

I'm so effing happy and grateful, now that I'm happy and grateful and living my perfect life in my perfect home, perfect kids, perfect everything. I love my life! I write as I'm trying to remember to remember to have faith.

Blog Post

Voltaire: "Faith consists of believing when it's beyond the power of reason to believe." Today has been a hard day for me. Yesterday a friend gave me the book, The Geography of Bliss by Eric Weiner; One Grumps Search for the Happiest Places in the World, and for those of you who are new to my blog, this was my dream. This is what I've been searching for and what I've been wanting to do – travel to all the happiest places in the world and then write about it.

I haven't disclosed much on my blog about my personal life, and that's because my last ten, no twenty years have been hell. I've been knocked down so many times I can't count, so much that I'm writing a book about it. It's too much to describe in just a few short sentences. My blog has been my thoughts of things I want to remember. What I need to hear and read when I get down, and it has worked. I'm being more productive, and I'm working toward the goals that I hoped would lead me to my dream, and I hope that it's helping you too.

I describe myself as a displaced worker. I've been self-employed for the last fifteen years, and I've put all my funds into ventures that now in this economy are obsolete. I've been living off my savings and then sold assets and am waiting for my now largest asset to sell. If it sells, I won't really see any large profit, I just won't have to declare bankruptcy. So, one way or another I should be out of debt in a few months from now.

I am also a single mom, and I'm trying to hold it together for my children. My son is at the local community college, and I'm not really worried about him. He is brilliant, low maintenance, works and supports himself. I believe he will be just fine. My youngest will be graduating high school this spring and wants to be a doctor.

She has taken all the right steps to get into a good school; she deserves to attend a good school. But at this point I don't even know if I'm going to have a roof over my head, much less how I'm going to be able to help her go to school. She's applying, but we'll just have to wait and see how it all turns out. No pressure!

My plan was/is to write my blog, get healthier mentally and physically, and hopefully grab some readers along the way, and somehow earn some money, while I write my memoir. All the while, getting through *this mess of my life, then taking my daughter to college, and spend the rest of my life traveling, writing, and blogging. I wanted to write a book on the happiest places in the world – I need happy!*

So, if you're coming to my blog because your life is shit too… and you're looking for a way to get through the tough times then just know that I get it. But, let's try and stay positive, have faith that somehow, we'll have the life that we'd dream.

I still want to travel to all the happiest places in the world, I'll just have to write about something else.

Just a thought!
With Love,
Goldi
GoldilocksBlog.com
Having the perfect life in a perfect world ;)

Yoga and Meditation Practice

Journal Entry

I'm forgetting to have faith that the universe is working for me. I need to remember that sometimes the story that we're heading for is often to lead us in another direction. Maybe to wake us up to what's right in front of us. I guess the anger and sadness is the old me speaking and feeling and reacting and not the me I want to be. What does it matter if 20 people have written a book about it if it's what I want to do? Shouldn't I just do it for the pure pleasure of doing it. Am I getting lost in my poor me story again?

Positive Statement Set in the Present Tense

I'm so grateful now that my children are in a great place in their lives and we are all happy and healthy. I'm so blessed. I have a man who knows me in a very deep and real way without me having to tell him. I believe and have faith that everything just works out for me. I have a great love and a stable secure home. I have the perfect blend of stable home life and a life of adventure while traveling and writing. I take care of myself now more than ever. I work out, practice yoga, and take long walks in nature. I feel great! And, remarkably I have enough time for everything.

Blog Post – Perfection

I always look back at my last blog post, before I write my next, and rereading the post made me cringe a bit. Which brings me to today's point: we may never reach that ultimate level of perfection in anything that we do. And, if we wait to know that we'll do it perfectly before taking action then we may never try anything. So, go sound "cheesy." Do something sloppily but do it! Whatever "it" is for you! Just make that first move.

Just a thought…
Love, Goldi
GoldilocksBlog.com
Having the perfect life in a perfect world…

DONNA MELANSON

Circa 2010

My life continued in this back and forth pattern of positive and negative thoughts sometimes daily and at times hourly, but the negative talk became less and less, and the positive talk became more and more. My good days I've noticed are always on the days when I've practiced yoga. It grounds me and keeps me in the present moment, not in what I've become bitter about and not what I'm afraid of what will happen.

And, then Mike came around. Mike was my brother's childhood friend. I had messaged him right after my brother had a heart attack. My brother was bored since he was supposed to rest for a while. I told him about Facebook, he wasn't on it yet. I had just joined and was having a lot of fun getting in touch with all my old friends now that I had more free time.

I talked him into joining and suggested "friends" for him to connect with, and one of them was Mike. Mike and I began chatting and catching up on life. He was going to be coming up my way with his two sons, and his ex-brother and sister-in-law, to visit their mountain house in Tennessee.

I wasn't surprised when he called from his car on his way up saying he was passing through my town. I asked where he was, and he was just approaching my exit. I was in the car heading to the grocery store that was right at the exit and told him to get off so that we could say hi. He was in a convoy with his ex-brother and sister-in-law and didn't think he could make it happen.

A few days later Mike called and asked if I wanted to come over for a cookout. I wasn't sure as it was an hour away and he had just driven right by me. Ally however was gone on a week-long camping trip, so I said to myself – why not.

Why else would anyone drive an hour to go see their brothers' friend that you haven't seen in over twenty years, at his ex-brother and sister-in-law's house with all the children?

At first it was awkward as he greeted me with a friendly kiss, because you know me the one who cries by being touched by a masseuse. I have that social distance thing that I'm comfortable with. He introduced me to Kaylynn and Paul, his ex-brother and sister-in-law and their son Ben and then to his son's David, and Thomas.

Mike told me that his youngest daughter Caitlyn is the same age as Ally, and she stayed home to work. He also has an older daughter, Christine, who lives in Kentucky with her three sons. He then gave me a tour of the house and on our way up the stairs I felt a light tap on my butt. I'm not sure if he meant to do it or not.

The surprising part of it all was that I felt an energy of some kind with just that quick light touch that had me on alert. I thought I was going to see my brother's friend and he never mentioned any type of attraction to me, but this jolt of electricity had me totally off my game.

We headed outside to the back porch where his ex-brother-in-law is and sat down to chat. Mike's boys are sitting inside, along with Ben and they were having fun looking out at us through the window. We chat for over an hour before its time to eat, but Mike made me mad after I told him a little bit of my story, and that I'm seriously considering joining the peace corp.

He said it sounded "desperate." I was instantly defensive. I thought it was a brilliant plan. I'd realized over the last few months that when Ally goes off to school that I'm finally going to make choices for me. I'm no longer looking for a man. I feel like this is a great opportunity to travel, I could help people, and in the evenings

I could write. I'd already been looking into it and had attended a meeting. But I had wondered why I had not committed already.

As we headed into dinner that Kaylynn had been graciously been preparing. Mike and I playfully banted back and forth and, I felt that energy again. Then and maybe because of that or whatever is going on, Kaylynn called me her future sister-in-law. I just came to say hi, but for some strange reason after dinner, I didn't want to leave.

Mike called me a couple of days later and asked if I want to give him a tour of downtown, and a few days after that he picked me up. We went on a walking tour and popped into a few microbreweries. We were really enjoying ourselves and as we headed back to his car, he opened up the door for me and we both lingered.

I don't know what he was thinking but I was wondering what's going on. I'm feeling more and more of an attraction for him, but it feels weird because he's my brother's friend. I think we both wanted to move forward and kiss. However, I stepped into the car, and Mike walked around to the other side and drove us to my mom and nono's rental home that Ally and I are now living in.

We went inside to chat, and I'm felt more and more of an attraction for him, and when he said goodbye, we do kiss. The next day he drove home to Florida. We kept chatting and then we began having virtual dinner dates, with each of us fixing our own meals, while at our own homes, located eight hundred miles apart, staring at each other through the computer screens, getting to know each other more.

We meet up only two more times in person before deciding that we were going to live together at his home in Florida, along with his children Caitlyn, David, and Thomas. Ally is going off to school. Since life was serving me up a clean plate it only made sense for me to move to him. I always wanted to have a big family, and now I feel like I do.

Its mind blowing for me to think that if I hadn't lost everything I would never have been on Facebook, and therefore, I never would have looked for Mike. I never would have been able to move my life. I would have been fully entrenched in a life, that I did not enjoy living.

And, then some other surprising things began to happen. Not only did it seem crazy to me that at the very moment that I was free in every sense of the meaning, without a job, home, and no longer needing to be a full-time parent as my daughter was heading to college, I find the love of my life, but then I lost access to my email account.

The email account with over three thousand contacts that were attached to my old life. I tried all my passwords to no avail, and I was unable to convince Gmail that the account was mine.

I was, however, still logged in through my phone, so I was still able to access it all, until with just a few little drops of water, a few months later, I lost my phone, my email, and all my phone contacts too. It was as if the universe was saying let go. Let go of your old life already! What do I have to do to you, to get you to let go? So, I did, I let it all go.

Goldilocks Blog - "About Me" Update

Circa 2011

Wow, it's been over two years since I started my blog, and I've been thinking that it's time to update my "About Me" section, and after reading it. I can't believe how far I've come, and how remarkable it is that I've received everything I've been looking for in my "just right" life, except, maybe, not exactly in the way I was envisioning it.

For example, I've had so many friends and family around me, which is awesome, but when you've come from a drought, it's felt like a sudden, heavy rain shower that's lasted for days, leaving you feeling totally unprepared. When what I was imagining of was more of a steady drizzle that keeps you sustained, but it's perfect just the way it is.

I talked of traveling and in the last month I've been to the city of Santiago, and the desert of San Pedro de Atacama, Chile, where I stayed in Hostels, and sand boarded in the desert. I saw a beautiful cactus forest and spent time in a natural hot spring. I walked on the vast and seemingly never-ending salt flats.

I stood lake side as the sun was setting, with an awe-inspiring view of the volcanic mountains in the distance mimicked back by the reflection on the lake, while watching hundreds of pink flamingos fly overhead. And, viewed many other magnificent sunsets while standing at the grand canyons and valleys. At night I was in awe as I look up at more stars than I'd ever thought I'd see. Where just being there really made you feel that grateful energy of being alive.

We then toured the southern states of the USA going through Florida, Georgia, South Carolina, North Carolina, Kentucky, Alabama and seeing a city with the coolest tag line as we drove by; Boaz Alabama, The city of Possibilities. I then ended my travels that year in the white sands of Bimini Bahamas, where we relaxed and snorkeled and swam in the turquoise waters, in what seemed like our own life-size fishbowl.

And, I did find that love that I'm sure will last a lifetime. He's exactly what I imagined my prince to be. He's handsome, kind, caring, compassionate, loving, brings me coffee in bed, and says he will always love and take care of me know matter what "I promise, I promise, I promise."

And you know what? I didn't have to tell him my story, He knew my family, and he had been through some of his own stuff that gave him clear insight into what I'd been through. When I met him, I didn't have to wonder if he was the right one for me. I'd been writing about him for a year, in my positive statements that I set in the present tense. So, when he asked me to marry him, it was easy to say yes.

In all the changes and in settling myself into my new life I begin writing a little less and started studying yoga more and more. In fact, I'm becoming a yoga teacher. It's that same internal deep nudge from within that I had with writing. Like my life cannot take another path until this mission is done. I'm listening.

And, I hope you are too.
Love, Goldi

PART THREE

BE YOURSELF

A Yogi's Path to Peace

BE YOURSELF

Circa NOW

The following pages are a continuation of my growth as I moved along the path of a yogi, which begins where, for the first time, I'm meeting myself exactly where I am. The path to peace begins by knowing yourself in a deep soul satisfying way.

Yoga is the settling of the mind into silence, tapping into who we are at our soul level, our connection to all, and it is here for us in this moment, and then the next and the next. When you sit in the silence and stillness you begin to tap into this awareness of who you are. You feel your connection to the whole, and you begin to have more awareness of those intuitive nudges from within, the whispers, the voices, the internal drive that guides you.

Yoga isn't just what you see in media, a series of physical postures but it is more than that. It's the union of the body and mind fully present in the moment, and we can tap into some of this when doing other things that we are totally immersed in.

Potters feel the clay between their fingers, as they become one with the clay that they mold and shape. A runner is in tuned with their step as each foot touches the earth, in tune to the natural rhythm of motion. And, the best surfer is one with the waves, the tide, the ocean.

When the body and mind is settled through the physical postures or through the breath, it then becomes much easier to be fully present in the moment. Aware of awareness, then detaching with awareness of what is. Aware of your thoughts, aware of your ego, aware of your beliefs and habits. The more you practice in this mindful way, the more you learn about yourself and the world around you.

As I begin stepping into my role as a teacher, I continue my journaling, my positive statements set in the present tense, which I learn that the way I was practicing them, is called a sankulpa. Where you put a deeper meaning behind the statements, more of a knowing that what you're saying is the present truth, even if you can't see it yet. That's your intention for your life. Your belief is what you become. You get what you expect.

I'm a different person now. My life flows better, and every day I discover more and more of who I really am, and who I'm meant to be. It took me almost fifty years but that's okay I'm grateful for the discovery, for the peace, for happiness.

It's interesting that the path is always easier to see when you look at someone else's life, or when you look back at your own. Now I've found this clarity in the present moment, when I meditate, I know I'm on the right path.

Thoughts

- Every day I do something that is good for my mind, body, and soul.
- Every day I remember that energy within me and outside of me is always available to me.
- Every day I reaffirm in my mind, what it is that I wish to create.
- Every day I know that all things are possible.
- Every day I believe that the universe is working for me.

Circa 2012

I'm practicing yoga four times a week as a yoga teacher trainer. I don't do it every day yet like I want it to. In my studies of yoga through awareness and stillness, I've found that it leads you to an effortless way of living in the world. I wonder if that's what our quest in life should be, to truly know ourselves, and then to live from that place of knowing.

Are we so conditioned that we need to meditate and quiet the chatter of the perceived life around us, getting us quiet and still, so that we can wake up to our true selves? Then having to remember to have faith, as you take the steps that lead you in the direction of the life you want to live, as you listen to the voice inside.

Positive statement set in the present tense and Journal Entry

In my heart I know that everything is taken care of. I flow through life with ease and grace. I wake up in the morning and take care of my body and mind. I write words that by grace will help others. I teach yoga and the words and practice helps to enrich the lives of others. I have more than enough. I help others. I have great friends. I have a great family. I truly have a great and blessed life.

This is what I'm meditating on daily, then placing my mind within my heart to carry on into the day. I've created a mantra that I use daily; *I am happy, I am healthy, I am whole, I am love, I am*

A YOGI'S PATH TO PEACE   177

light, *I flow through life with ease and grace.* Often tacking on *good things always come my way!*

I see myself teaching in the morning, then writing after, and then carrying on with LOVE, LOVE, LOVE, all around me. What a great life!

Goldilocks Blog Post

Begin by loving yourself! Treat yourself how you want others to treat you. Know what you want. Envision what it looks like. Embody what it feels like. And believe!

Goldilocks Blog Post

Strength in Change

When major changes happen in your life, even when the change is to improve your life, it can make you feel a little unsettled and distressed. So, when life forces you to change, and you think the change is catastrophic, it can seem debilitating, but it's really what makes us stronger.

Just like an analogy I heard once, that if an egg is broken from the outside, life ends, but if broken from the strengthening efforts made by the baby chick, life begins. All of our strength comes from within. We must do our own inside work.

Pay attention to your thoughts, pay attention to what to you say to yourself and others; observe, be the witness, have awareness. If you think you're defeated, you will never take the necessary steps. Which is why we're often defeated before we begin. What we think and what we believe makes it so.

If the mind wanders you must remember to shift your thoughts from what's happened in the past and what your fearing the future may bring to what it is that you want to create. If you find your mind continually wandering begin to start using the words however, or, nevertheless I don't how, but it's possible. Remember to remember that you're only going to focus on the remarkable outcome that could possibly occur. Focus on the positive.

This is your inside work. This is your new focus – surrender and say, Somehow, I'm growing stronger, and the universe is working in my favor, bringing me everything I need and everything I don't even know that I need.

Just a thought…
Love, Goldi

———— ⁓⁓⁓⦿⦿⦿⁓⁓⁓ ————

Goldilocks Blog Post

"If you want to improve, be content to be thought foolish and stupid." Epictetus

You don't really know what you're capable of. Have the courage to do something different – adapt and change. Be fearless, talk to people about it. Step up, step out and be noticed, try new things, and expect more.

If you don't try, you will never know.

Just a thought…
Love, Goldi

Goldilocks Blog Post - Gratitude of Breath

Meditate a moment with gratitude of all that you have to be grateful for, starting with your breath. I said that, this past weekend, at the end of teaching my very first yoga class. Because in yoga, and in life, we begin and end with breath.

We often forget that and get caught up in the drama of what's going on around us, we forget to pause, we forget that we have anything to be grateful for, when really "the breath" should be enough.

I believe we often overlook the things that come so easy to us, and how often that they are usually our greatest gifts.

Think for a moment about the gift of sight, of touch, to feel, to taste, to hear, to heal, to think. If anyone of these were the newest invention, how badly would you want them?

And, you do!!

Then, think about some other gifts you have that are unique to you.

See - you're amazing, and you didn't even have to do anything.

Meditate on that - on just how amazing you are, just as you are!

Sit in gratitude.

Just a thought...
Love, Goldi

In my yoga teacher training, I've developed this intuitive nudge from within to practice yoga every morning at sunrise, much like the intuitive nudge that guided me to write, and to take yoga teacher training in the first place. Like it's something that I just have to do.

Because of my years of self-study, I know myself enough now to know that I wouldn't do that for just myself, so I teach for over a year three mornings a week at 6:30 am for free at the yoga studio that I've taken my training with.

I continue my yoga studies while teaching classes, with advanced training in Meditation, Yoga Nidra, Vedic Thai Yoga, Restorative Yoga, a 500-hour Yoga Teacher training, Children's Yoga and Prenatal Yoga. But It wasn't until I finished all the trainings that I could possibly have, we moved, and we moved closer to the beach. A dream that Mike and I both had.

We had been looking for a new house for some time waiting for the right situation, and then it appeared, and we quickly had to act to make it all come together. It wasn't until we'd been living in our new home for four months when I realized that I'd not been to the beach, not once. I had however been envisioning and feeling the essence of the serenity of being on the beach and listening to ocean sounds as I breathed in salt air for years.

I had no longer been teaching the early morning yoga class, but that intuitive nudge from within was still there to practice daily at sunrise. So, I declared that I was going to start taking myself to the beach every day at sunrise to practice a little yoga and meditation. Finally getting myself to the beach and fulfilling the internal nudge that I had for three years.

This was part of the perfect life I had been envisioning and was still creating, as I had not changed my pattern of positive statements and journaling, although I may not have been as consistent in the writing, but it was always present in my mind. I had this desire to practice yoga, to help inspire people, to get to this place of peace that I now feel every day.

The beach is so beautiful at sunrise. Every day I went to the same spot at the beach, but every day was so different. Somedays the ocean was calm and still, and the next day it could have giant waves, and often it was somewhere in between. The shoreline was different too with the ocean tide leaving me with an expansive beach or just the right amount.

The clouds, the wind and the sunrise were all different too as I gratefully witnessed mother nature's daily show. I sat in awe of the beauty of nature as the sun rose and the light glistened across the water towards me. I listened to the soothing sounds of the ocean and witnessed its natural ebb and flow that continued to repeat, effortlessly flowing in and out.

As I continued to sit in meditation, I became visually aware of how fast time goes by as I watched the sun rise higher and higher in the sky. I felt a strong connection to all things. It's the same feeling I had on the mountain, but a different kind of energy, like a cleansing, a renewal. Whereas on the mountain I felt grounded, nurtured, and nourished with a deep connection. I believe we need places like this and time to pause, to remind us of our connection to all.

The beach at sunrise continued to inspire me by its awe-inspiringly beautiful images, that I felt that I needed to share it with others. It was just too beautiful to keep to myself. So, I started posting photos to Instagram, along with an inspiring thought, daily. Wendy, a fellow yoga teacher who lived on the beach said she had been seeing me on the beach practicing daily and felt compelled to tell me that I should start broadcasting LIVE on periscope.tv.

She said it's a new cool app owned by Twitter. I listened because it was an intuitive nudge from within her, that led her to tell me.

Reluctantly however, not wanting to take on any more social media tasks, and because of being a natural introvert, I put off broadcasting for a month.

My broadcast, at first, showed mostly the view because I thought that's what would inspire people most. However, the more I broadcasted the more people wanted to know more about me and what I did for a living, which led me to start sharing with everyone my morning yoga and meditation practice. The hour-long broadcast which I'm still at the time of this writing doing daily, 7 days a week for five years now, always starts off with, *Good Morning, Good Morning, Good Morning you beautiful souls. It's another beautiful day in South Florida, another beautiful day to pause for peace. Peace for your body, peace for your mind, peace for your soul, peace for the world.*

I greet people as they begin joining the broadcast. We chat a bit then we practice a little yoga and meditation. We chat some more and occasionally some interesting and incredible things happen, besides the daily views of the ocean at sunrise, the yoga and meditation.

For example, when I first started broadcasting, I brought my phone close to the ocean to show everyone how clear the water is and a viewer wrote into the broadcast, *"Be careful, don't drop your phone."* Right while I was dropping my phone into the water. Okay maybe that wasn't interesting or incredible, but it was recorded LIVE.

Another example is the time after a hurricane I found a giant two-foot-wide by over three-foot-long sea sponge that I somehow rescued. I placed it on my yoga mat and then dragged it down the beach while still broadcasting. You cannot believe how heavy a wet sponge of this size weighs. I could barely move it. And a whole comedy ensued where the viewers of the broadcast improvised a whole story about the struggle.

A man stopped me and asked me what I was doing, I showed

him, but to the viewers who couldn't see everything, they filled in the blanks writing in, *"Run, hide, they're going to get you. Don't let him see the body."* The man did look at me like I was crazy as I dragged this very heavy sea sponge on my yoga mat. Luckily for me, since I broadcast early in the morning, there weren't too many people at the beach, or I probably would have been reported for something.

The highlight of my morning beach meditation was being approached by the Secretary-General of Religious Leaders, Bawa Jain. He had been traveling to Boca Raton, Florida on the weekends to help a sick friend, and while he was in Boca, he was heading to the beach at sunrise daily to meditate. He'd seen me at the beach the week before, and I had also noticed him meditating. He was more than gracious and agreed to be on my broadcast, sharing, educating, and inspiring us all.

Soon, I was trending on Periscope.tv and was featured several times on the app. The publicity grew my audience and led me to be selected to teach two meditation classes at the prestigious Yoga Journal Live event in Hollywood, Florida. Then later through the introduction of Bawa Jain, at the next Yoga Journal LIVE event in New York City, I was able to give Deepak Chopra a hug on his behalf.

My life continues to unfold for me in this miraculous manner now. I have thousands and thousands of followers all over the world, and I get to spread peace, love and good energy daily through my broadcast. I'm inspiring other people just like I had desired all those years ago.

I don't want anyone to ever feel the way I did, which is why I do what I do, including writing this book. I hope my journey helps because I want to remind you - *it works* - the yoga, the meditation and the shift into a positive mindset. It may or may not all happen totally like you want; it may end up better. If you allow it to be, and don't get lost in the details.

For me, this is my book ten years in the making. But I told myself that there must be a reason for the delay. It must just not have been the right time. So, I've been having faith that it will all work out perfectly, for the benefit of all. In the meantime, I'm happily writing this part of my story as I sit in my home in Bimini, Bahamas, a home that my husband had always wanted to build.

It overlooks the white sand beach and beautiful crystal-clear blue waters, just like the sand and water in my VHS video I watched daily of the gentle yoga class years ago. Is it all just a coincidence? I don't think so.

That nudge from within to write this book has never wavered, that drive from within to teach this practice, and share how to live happily, has never wavered. Guiding people to a place of peace, so that anyone who does this practice can find the love within, has never wavered.

I believe in it so much that's been driving factor behind my broadcasts because I want others to feel the way that I do now. That's how much I believe in it, and how much I know it to be true. The coolest part for me is that it's not like a job but it is what propels me to keep going. A knowing that it's a part of something greater than me.

When we meditate and sit in silence, we begin to have awareness of judgments and assumptions; awareness as to the stories that we tell ourselves, about ourselves, about other individuals, or countries, or races, or movies, or books, our awareness of all things. We start paying attention to what we are saying and begin having awareness of where those thoughts come from. Where do your judgements stem from, where did you learn the so-called rules?

You become aware that if you weren't born into the family you were born into, you may have another religion, another nationality, a different race, or you may not exist at all. You will become aware of how we're all connected on this planet, in this world. It's with this awareness of our connection to all things that we learn to do, to be, and to act in a certain way; a way that is honest and truthful to ourselves and to the world around us.

I want you to know that if you practice daily, believe, and surrender to the unlimited possibilities, your life will change and will get better and better. You will begin to remind yourself just like I have, and still do, to mind your thoughts and to live in this awareness.

You will begin to come into a greater sense of fulfillment every day. I want you to be inspired by how far I've come since the stories of my childhood, my marriage, my divorce, and my search for love and peace. The narrative that I told myself before, the story that I began to tell myself when I wanted my life to change, and what my life looks like now, and acknowledge the real distinction between the three. I want you to know that if you change your story, your life will change too.

You will have to start doing things differently, you will have to make new choices, you will have to overcome your current way of thinking and being. If you can understand this, and you are able to do this, more possibilities will begin to open up to you as a result. You'll start to see all kinds of things start to happen for you and your life.

Start by doing a daily practice of yoga and meditation, of writing positive statements in the present tense, while feeling that good things are here for you now. This power of belief is everything! This belief begins to change not only you, but the world around you. When you begin to remember with awareness, your perception changes, you begin to fully understand, control and master the outcome of who you are and who you are becoming.

When you practice this daily, your subconscious mind which understands far more than you can consciously compute, will guide you and you will listen, which brings me back to the awareness of the family you were born into. Often, we move through life without this awareness, becoming without much thought, what we've observed in our daily life; from teachers, parents, friends, neighbors.

Most of us interact in the same way as the people around us and we don't realize it, unless we *remember to remember* and change the things we can control, which are our thoughts and actions. If we *remember to remember* to consciously do things differently, to practice peace daily, to meditate, to see clearly, we can become more of the beautiful and unique being that we are meant to be.

Not that I'm saying that you're not great as you are now, but I'm saying that you, yourself, can become the true version of you. Just like I did. I feel totally me. The true me, not the version that I was molded into but the version I was meant to be.

Begin your practice by becoming aware of who you are right now, and the story that you are telling yourself right now. Be aware that it's not always about the family, nationality, religion, something that our parents did or what they taught us, that creates us. It's also often a misunderstanding from childhood, like kids making fun of you of over something silly, like maybe something you're wearing something unusual, and their comment makes you feel bad about yourself. Or maybe it was a teacher or parent that made an off handed comment that's attached to how they were raised and doesn't have anything really to do with you, but you've owned that comment for years. A comment like, "You don't belong in this group," or "You're not good in math."

We often hold onto these comments forever, so developing the awareness to notice and study oneself, including how we react to things, then remembering to remember that it was just a comment. We don't know what's going on in their life.

Often when people say mean and unhelpful things it doesn't really have anything to do with you; it could be ignorance, a sick child, or worry about finances that makes them react in this manner, or it may be their true belief, but it doesn't have to be yours.

Be aware that all of it now are just stories that they have told and that we now tell ourselves over and over again. Let go of the emotional attachment to the words of the story. It happened and it sucked but it's in the past and we cannot change it. So, for your own wellbeing, you have to let it go.

A little caveat: when you're doing all the right things in life, and you feel like you are the good person and your life still isn't changing, or catastrophe happens, and it feels like the end of the world as we know it. Know that there is more than your energy in the universe. That's why bad things can happen to good people.

We must, however, do the work on ourselves, so at all times when other energies are also at play, which they always are, that we not only handle them with ease and grace but we're often less affected by them. Like being close to a cell phone tower, giving you great reception.

I often explain it like this in the most basic of ways because I know it sounds a little woo-woo. But I don't think that there is a better time for all of us to understand and get this. Energy is what allows me to wirelessly broadcast LIVE from the beach in Boca Raton, Florida, and for thousands of people from all over the world to wirelessly receive it.

My phone with my unique number gives one individual signal, sending to individuals on every continent at their home, in the park, or wherever, while simultaneously hundreds of thousands of people are on the same app looking at different broadcasters, while they receive it at their own unique location.

All of this happens, while the person next to all of those people are on a totally different app or maybe streaming a movie. We don't see the frequency moving toward each individual, and yet we all carry our own unique vibration. So just remember that energy is out there, as everything is energy. We don't have to see it. we just need to remember it's real and it works.

The same is true in our lives as we bring awareness to our own frequency. And, just like we have the ability to get a new phone number, where we're no longer able to receive calls with our old phone number, our frequency can change. And, just like my broadcast that's able to send a signal around the world, our energy is broadcasting all around us and can be felt around the world.

So, if you want to make a difference in the world, then do your best to change your energy to one of kindness, compassion and love. Remember this if you're putting someone else down, or being negative in any way, you're not only hurting yourself but the collective energy. We must be mindful of what we are broadcasting, and what we tune into.

Have awareness that the energy of a full moon makes the ocean rise. The planets, the moon, the stars, all are affecting us on some level. Have awareness that the energy of the family we are born in to affects our path and how we live. Have awareness that we have the ability to change our energy.

We have to have the courage to change, not only for ourselves but for everyone around us. We are not limited. Energy is everything. We have the energy within us, and we have the collective energy of those around us, so when you do your work, and I've done my work, we can help make a difference in the lives of many.

We don't have to have it totally figured out, we don't have to see it with our own eyes, but we do have to have the awareness that everything is connected. We're all really connected. To change your life, you must have this awareness. We must do our part to bring about the life we want to live and our part to receive good energy.

We have to be it, being who we truly are at our soul level, being who we are meant to be. Not wanting, or wishing, or desiring but *being* - making sure and believing that good is coming our way. It will allow for us to have the best possible outcome.

We've all experienced that time in our lives, like in mine, where bad things kept happening over and over. Some perpetuated by thoughts and feelings, like in my case throughout this story, and some by universal forces greater than us, like what is happening in the world right now, as I write in 2020, with this global pandemic.

Our lives ebb and flow. Going back to the line, flowing above and below. We want to be at our highest vibration so that we can ride this ebb and flow with ease and grace. Allowing the highs and lows to reach a higher level instead of hovering below the line where you never really rise above the sadness.

Two years ago, a suspicious spot showed up on my mammogram, which resulted in a biopsy and lumpectomy. I was then in a car accident, and because of my car accident when my six-month checkup showed something else that needed to be biopsied, I had to put it off because I was still in pain from the car accident.

When that six months came up, I no longer feeling I could put it off, I had another biopsy and subsequent lumpectomy on the same breast. Then six months later still hurting from the car accident, my neurosurgeon recommended a cervical spinal fusion on two levels of my spine, because the spinal cord was being raked across bone.

I'm telling you all this because throughout these life challenges that still happen, I kept my yoga practice up, although it was a very gentle physical practice, but I did the breathing and the meditation which allowed me to be happy and at peace even though I was often tired and hurting. And, isn't that the goal of everyone, to be happy?

Be an observer of your own experience. Look what's happening in your life as an indication of what's going on in your heart, your mind, your soul, in the very essence of your being. Study yourself and know what's happening beneath the surface. How does your body feel?

What thoughts are circling around your head? We believe with feeling, and we want to feel good, so be the observer, notice, witness, and change the thoughts that will change the feelings, that will change the beliefs, that will lead you to a happy life.

The benefits of my life after practicing yoga continue to flow better from the teachings of Patanjali. An ancient sage in India who live around three-thousand years ago, where we're guided to a place where we truly know ourselves in a deep way that allows us to feel whole.

As we begin this practice of the study of the self, the Yoga Sutras that Patanjali wrote teach us many lessons, that help guide us along our way. Beginning with nonviolence to our fellow man, and to the animals who roam this earth, but also practicing nonviolence to ourselves; by physically and mentally treating ourselves and every living being on this planet with loving kindness, and compassion. Paying attention to what we say and by meeting all situations with this loving awareness.

Live being truthful in your thoughts, speech and actions, thinking not only what is best for yourself, but what is best for the whole. Let go of feelings of lack, and of not having enough. When you meditate you begin to have an awareness of your true soul, the beautiful human being that is you.

Live in this Goldilocks state, that is unique to you, of not having too much or too little of something, which with awareness is fulfilling in itself. And, by finding understanding, and distancing ourselves less and less with what society dictates our desires should be in the attachment to worldly goods and figuring out what it is that we truly want.

Developing a feeling of knowing that you will be provided for, while making efforts along your path. In the sense that as you are sitting still doing nothing, you don't know what conversations are taking place or what email has been sent, or an intention or action of another person. Simply trust that the universe is working for your benefit. Keep going and have faith.

Our frustrations in life are often exacerbated by our reactions to them, which my own story can attest to. A negative reaction makes it harder to find the balance needed for peace. We create our own suffering by the stories we tell ourselves. Learn to change your focus.

Study yourself and develop awareness of what's going on within you and all around you. Feed your mind with thoughts of gratitude.

Feed your mind with positive information, and know thyself, in a deep, deep way.

Have the clarity of mind that comes from meditation, and from cleanliness that goes beyond our possessions, but also to the cleanliness of thoughts, by letting go of the thoughts that do not serve us. Which can be one of the hardest tasks to master.

I had a friend with a small child and the when the child didn't want something she would shake her head back and forth and say no, no, no. I took on this inner child of mine, and when I found myself thinking negative thoughts, I would see that child in my mind shaking her head and saying no, no, no. Allowing me to let go of the negative thought. You'll need to develop your own system of how to shift your thoughts, but I thought I would share what worked for me.

Develop an overall purity of the body, honor yourself in all ways. Eat healthy, exercise moderately, and rest when needed. This is essential not only for the function of our nervous system, but it's essential for our overall well-being. Know when disappointment comes, that something good will happen from what feels like a sacrifice of letting go.

Always show up and do the best you can with what you have, where you are, and then surrender to the outcome. Sit in the satisfaction of a job well done. You may not ever find out what you've been spared, or what good has come your way from it; show up anyway and do your best.

Strengthen your body to free energetic and muscular tension, starting from wherever you are with no judgments, just simply show up, again and again. Just doing the best you can with what you have where you are. Practice being mindful in every moment unifying the body, mind, and soul, living in the present moment.

This is the key, because if you're already physically fit but your mind is racing, then you're only getting part of what you need. Just as if you are fully present, but have no comfort when you sit, you'll not be able to sustain your meditation. According to the yoga sutras you should be steady and comfortable, aware of your strength and your peace.

In the practice of yoga, we reduce obstacles and strengthen the nervous system, by practicing strengthening our body and our breath.

Breath and thought go together. We can slow down the thoughts by focusing on the breath, being aware of the sensation and the sound, the rhythm and the texture - turning inward.

Holding this concentration and steadying the mind - one pointed focus. And when this flow is uninterrupted you establish a connection. It is here with a quiet mind that you discover an understanding of all things. This is where happiness begins.

When we begin living in this certain way, in whatever way it that it uniquely looks like for us. Maybe, it's to write a positive book, to raise children in a happy household, or to become President of our country. Every job is important, and we're all called to do certain things. We all win, when we show up and do our best and do it with the intention of doing something better for the whole.

Begin a daily practice to help you remember. Make it a ritual or something that you do like brushing your teeth and eating lunch. Make it an essential part of your day. You never want life to go back to the way it was, and because when you practice, you get good at what you practice, and you no longer want to be that angry, stressed person. You want to be happy and you want to live in peace.

My method is to at a minimum begin your practice grounding in the present moment. Aware of where you physically are. Aware of the sounds around you near and in the distance. Aware of the rise and fall of the breath. Noticing the sensation of the breath, sound of the breath, the rhythm of the breath. Then begin a few mindful movements linked with the breath, practice letting go, then sitting in stillness to meditate – just be.

Your mind needs to quiet, and your breathing needs to slow. Your mind and body are connected. In times of deep turmoil, you need more of a physical practice that includes breath work. In times of calm and peace we can do just a few gentle movements before settling down to meditate.

With a daily practice of meditation, we release stress and gain clarity of mind. Starting the day off in this way becomes just as important as taking a shower. It's about living in a healthy way of being.

There are many ways to practice yoga and meditation, just as many as there are types of food or chefs in the kitchen. Try many types and many teachers and find what works for you. You may also find as your life changes you'll probably need different ways of practicing yoga and meditation. Honor your body, honor your breath, honor life by honoring yourself.

We're all connected, and it's so clearly evident in the current climate that we're in; global pandemics, pollution in our sea and air. We even have information pollution for that matter. Never before have we been so clearly connected to the world around us. What affects you, affects the world.

We often consider ourselves small, and unimportant pieces in this grand scheme, but it's not true. Every being on this planet is equally important. We should live in a world where no one worries about food and shelter and has at a minimum all basic necessities of life, and every person should be expected to do their work on themselves and for themselves, and not be controlled mentally by the hand that they were dealt.

We must endeavor to show up and do our best with what we have where we are always. Often in the past we've judged our fellow man thinking that the person serving us is less than us. Like the person who picks up our trash. But can you imagine a world with no trash pick-up? I'm truly grateful that my trash is picked up every week and that it's not piling up around me.

We need the arts, we need the entertainment, we need the technology, and we need to honor and respect ourselves and to honor and respect all fellow human beings. We must begin to respect everyone's differences and recognize that we are all just human beings on this planet together, and then we can begin to heal nations and the world.

We talked earlier about the negative feelings that we feel and hold in our body, like the example of the jolt of tension you would get if someone walked into the room shouting. We can help the world, and directly all the people around us, by minding our own energy that we carry with us. That's why it's so important to do our own work. What heals us can help heal the world. If you can't do it for yourself, do it for everyone around you. The world is depending on it.

Be compassionate, you never know what another person has been through or is going through now. You probably feel like you've been through a lot, and that people don't fully understand what you've been through, and it's true – they don't. The truth is that everyone feels that way. Everyone has a story. So have compassion for all and extend that loving kindness out into the world.

Hang out with friends and inspire hope, be a positive energy so they can break out of that downward spiral too. See yourself fully present in the moment, aware of your emotions, choosing to respond

DONNA MELANSON

with what's happening around you with loving kindness, because it's the stories that you tell yourself, that keep you in the suffering, or frees you for the now.

You cannot change the past, you can only help the future, but only by truly living in the now, in a healthy happy way. And, the bonus is, that what we do for ourselves, we do for others. When we learn how to make ourselves happy, then everyone around us is lifted up. We are no longer part of the problem.

We have so much beauty in the world, we need to live in that state of appreciation; grateful to be alive. We can make life as good or as bad as we want by focusing our time and attention on love and loved ones, spending every day doing things that make us feel good, treating our self with love, kindness and compassion.

Remember to remember to help you live your best life is to continually refocus your mind, to find something good around you no matter how small it is, the flower of a weed, the sun shining overhead, or the fact that you are breathing. Be grateful in the moment and live in that way every day.

We begin living with the awareness of the infinite possibilities that can come, moving farther into that space of the possibilities of life. Believing in the good that's coming your way; surrender and keep moving forward. Keep showing up, being the best version of yourself in whatever beautiful way that looks like. I hope you love yourself. I hope you choose to love others. I hope that collectively we choose to love everyone around the world.

Believe in the unlimited possibilities of life and in the infinite potential you have. You have to believe it, you have to feel it, you have to know it on every level of your being as the truth

The more you practice awareness, and mindfulness, the more self-confident you will become in moving towards living your authentic life. And if we fall, we must get up, and start again. Yoga begins now in this moment, and then in this moment. Every moment of every day and so when we hear loud negative thoughts enter our minds, we must then just shake them off and begin again in this moment.

The more the self-defeating conversation is happening in your mind, the longer you will continue to feel the heaviness of your life. Your life is controlled more by what you think, what's in your heart, and it becomes a self-fulfilling prophecy.

Pay attention to what you are letting into your mind. Are you been programmed by the news, or is a neighbor's seed of fear being planted within your mind? Be aware of what is coming into your consciousness. Be aware of what's happening around you. What are you looking at or watching on TV?

What are you saying about yourself and about others? What are you listening too? What are you reading? What kind of energy are you putting into your body with those thoughts? Remember that what you put into your mind; you feel on every level of your being.

The mind is powerless to resist what is suggested to us, so start filling it up with good. The body is directed by the mind. Believe good is coming your way. We don't want to deny how we're feeling, but simply to have awareness. Suggesting to yourself that although you might not be feeling well today, you're going to focus what you can do for yourself to make you feel better right now in this moment. If the best you can do is sit on the coach and watch television all day, then do it. Have compassion for yourself and treat yourself with kindness. You are human, after all.

When you focus on all the negative, like I did, it's like saying to the universe that you don't appreciate all the good that you do have in your life, like the blue sky, the bird's sweet song, or the food you just consumed. Acknowledge all the good that's come your way and sit in the space of gratitude. The more we appreciate what we have the more we'll be given.

If you truly want to change your circumstances, you have to let go of whatever has happened in your life. You have to have awareness of your thought patterns and start refining the thoughts of your mind. Remember to remember to live in this way. Be willing to change. Be willing to try.

Be willing to give this practice a chance to see if this can make a difference in your life. Trust your instincts, be your own teacher, do your own work. And if you're willing to make the change in thoughts, your life like mine, will begin to change in miraculous ways.

Peace, joy and happiness are the goal, this is what you're searching for. Change your thoughts, get a new reality. Know yourself, love yourself, and be yourself, and give yourself permission to appreciate where you've been. It's what will make you sit in gratitude for the now peaceful happy being that you are.

Feel your greatness within as a beautiful soul fully present in the moment. Move into the silence and stillness, that the deep space of meditation with a knowing that you'll be living life in a more meaningful way. It becomes not about successes and failures, but about who you're becoming as you live through them. See yourself flowing through life with ease and grace, so that those moments of highs and lows, don't define the beautiful and unique being that is you.

My intention in sharing this story is to give hope that life can and will get better, and to share some tools and strategies to get you there. We need to live in a place where we love ourselves and every human being in the world. Love needs to be the driving factor for all.

———— ᴍᴏᴏᴇᴛᴏᴏᴛ౨ᴏᴏ·ᴍ ————

I'm going to end this story now like I end my LIVE broadcast with a meditation, in what the viewers have named our Circle of Love. They will often comment: "hands and paws in" and /or "joining hands and joining hearts," as we get ready to pause for peace.

Get in a comfortable seated position. Become aware of the support of the earth beneath you. Know, that the earth is supporting you right now in this moment. Allow it to take your weight, and have the awareness of how huge that is, that the earth is supporting you!

Sit up tall, and breathe in deeply, and exhale slowly. Taking a few nice long slow deep breaths in and out, breathing through the nose.

Be aware of the sensation of the breath.

The sound of the breath.

The rhythm of the breath.

Know that you are breathing and are alive with energy and vibration! Feel it on every level of your being as you take one more nice long slow deep breath in. Holding the breath at the top for just a moment. While keeping the length in your spine, rooting down from the tail bone up to the top of your head, and as you begin to exhale, relax the shoulders, relax the body, relax the mind.

Feel your strength and be aware of your peace, growing brighter and brighter with every breath. Breathing in Peace, breathing in Love, breathing in good energy and good vibrations. Know that you have the power to create this feeling of peace within you at any time.

And, because it feels so good to feel this way, we want to share it with everyone.

Using your mind and imagination I want you to see yourself sending peace and love and good energy out to the world, and because you are one of the people in the world, allow yourself to receive the good energy and vibrations that everyone is sending out.

Know that you're giving as one but receiving from many. Allow yourself to give fully and receive gracefully. With every breath you take just feel your heart grow bolder and brighter, filled with this love and light.

Let's continue to share this good energy and good vibrations of peace and love to everyone around us; friends and family, neighbors, and the people you don't know down the street.

Now, expand your sphere of good energy out further to include everyone in the country that your living in right now. Seeing love and light shower down upon everyone.

Then, see all of us join hands and join hearts as we circle the world for a global hug of peace and love.

Bring your hands together at your heart center, pausing here for a moment of gratitude; grateful for our bodies, our breath, our life. Grateful for this moment in time.

Then, take a moment to pause to think of at least three things you are grateful for.

May all of us be happy, healthy, and whole.
Aum shanti, shanti, shanti.
Aum meaning everything past, present, and future. Shanti meaning peace. May you have peace in the past. May you have peace in the present, and peace in the future.

Namaste!

Thank you for making it to this point in my book. We've come a long way! Before we leave our time together, I want you to take a moment to honor yourself for the beautiful and unique being that you are, just as you are.

Journal Entry

A gentle reader said as she read my book that it sounds like two different people wrote the book. It's true, I am different than I was.

End

DONNA MELANSON

Made in the USA
Las Vegas, NV
09 January 2024

84150253R00125